THE
A.R.V.I.S.
EFFECT

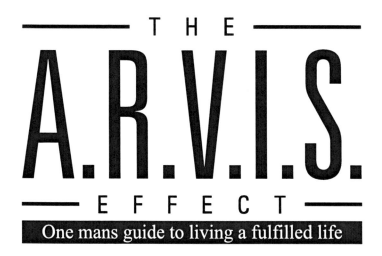

THE A.R.V.I.S. EFFECT

One mans guide to living a fulfilled life

Guy Michaels CH, CHt.

TATE PUBLISHING
AND ENTERPRISES, LLC

Published by Tate Publishing & Enterprises, LLC
127 E. Trade Center Terrace | Mustang, Oklahoma 73064 USA
1.888.361.9473 | www.tatepublishing.com

Tate Publishing is committed to excellence in the publishing industry. The company reflects the philosophy established by the founders, based on Psalm 68:11,

"The Lord gave the word and great was the company of those who published it."

Book design copyright © 2016 by Tate Publishing, LLC. All rights reserved.
Cover design by Dante Rey Redido
Interior design by Manolito Bastasa

Published in the United States of America

ISBN: 978-1-68270-874-3
Religion / Christian Life / Inspirational
16.07.12

To my family, friends, and all who have stood by me, believed in me, and supported me through the years. This book has been in the back of my mind for many years, and I have been running from it for an equal amount of time.

For those who are believers in Christ and who try to follow, to the best of our abilities, the example He set for us; you know that when we run from God, we actually end up running into God. That has happened to me many times in the contemplation of writing this book.

As you may have already suspected, God won.

Thank you all for loving me as I am—perfect in every way!

To Lisa, I am going to need some more paper!

Contents

Introduction

Hey, gang! I suppose at this point, an introduction is in order. My name is Guy Michael Smith, or simply, Guy Michaels—as most people know me these days. I am an ordinary man who has lived an extraordinary life so far. No, I have not walked on the moon or climbed Mount Everest. Nor have I cured cancer or found the fountain of youth. I've never driven a racecar or starred in a movie, and I have never had a hit song or set a world record. What I have done is lived a life full of good times, hard times, health, sickness, accomplishments, and challenges. Sound familiar? So what makes my story special? I have discovered a set of principles, which, if followed, will enable our lives to be an ultimate success. The definition of success may be different from person to person. That is what is so special about these principles! No matter what your definition of success is, you can attain the full and rich life you have always dreamed of! Guaranteed!

I would like to first clarify something to the readers of this book. I want you to know that I am a Christian man who has an ongoing relationship with the God of the Bible. The god of Abraham, Jehovah, I Am That, I Am. Jesus Christ , the second manifestation of God as God the Son, set an example for me (that I try) to follow every day. You are going to read about my experience(s) with God. You will see the name of Jesus throughout this book. If that offends you for some reason, that's okay! If you did not buy this book expecting to hear about God and want no part of it, that's okay too! Just visit www.guymichaels.net or www. thearviseffect.com and shoot me an e-mail. I will buy the book back from you no questions asked! However, I will not apologize for my relationship with God or for my faith in Jesus Christ. It is my choice, just as what you believe is yours. Hopefully the words to follow will strike a chord somewhere in your life as well. If not? That's perfectly okay too. You will receive *no* judgment from me!

So why should you read this book? What could I possibly have to share with you? I am not a celebrity or a politician or a world influence, so why should my words be taken seriously? Simply stated, I'm an ordinary person just like you. I've been through the wringer just like you. I've been "ridden hard and put up wet," just like you and I've come out on the other side stronger and better for it. I've experienced real-world problems that you face every day. Day-to-day issues—like paying the electric bill and the mortgage, family issues, or maintaining friendships with people who sometimes exhaust you—are important issues we all face daily that they can be tough! Putting your trust in God when faced with a life-threatening illness or "practicing what we preach" is much easier when we are offering advice to someone else. However, when it's *your* diagnosis that you are dealing with or the loss of *your* loved one, the game changes significantly. I've been there just like you!

Although I will go into my detailed testimony later in this book, I will say this:

I am a forty-eight-year-old, man from Texas. I've lived in four different states and have had an extraordinary, yet ordinary, life! I have faced my own mortality and have been told, "You should get your affairs in order prior to surgery!" Maybe some of you have not experienced my previous statement. If you have, you already know that being told something like that will separate your head from your shoulders! Figuratively speaking of course. If you have never had that conversation, I pray that you never do! I have been on the highest of the emotional and spiritual peaks and down in the lowest valleys, just like you!

Born to parents who cared more about being my parents first and my friend second, I was raised to do the right thing, even when no one is looking and you won't get credit for it. My father always told me this phrase, and it never really hit home until recently:

"Be the change that you want to see in the world.

Do what you feel in your heart is right regardless of popular opinion.

Serve others as best you can.

Remember, if you want more happy? Give it away!"

I will never forget those words!

There comes a time in everyone's life when you reach the point where you realize that there is much more to life than work, bills, deadlines, stuff, and things to keep our stuff in. When we reach that point, we learn that life is about quality and not quantity; it is only then we can truly be alive.

This book is not a story about the life of just one man. It's the culmination of years of observation, sampling, and implementation of a set of principles that were instilled in me, for years, without my knowledge. The teacher was not aware he was a teacher nor was he aware that the example he would set for me would have the life-changing effect it has. This man was not a scholar, educator, professor, world leader, inventor, philosopher, or critical mind. This man was not a leader of millions, world influence, or politician. This man was not known by the masses nor was he a celebrity.

This man was born in West Texas in 1940 and was a husband, son, brother, and a father to his sons. He was a hardworking man who was raised in a time where instant gratification was not the rule of the day. He was raised in a time when hard work and dedication to family was the way of the world.

This is not a biography of my father. It is a guide, a reference book, and a tool to help others live life according to the principles that he cemented into the minds of those he loved and in the minds of those who loved him. This is the ARVIS Effect.

1

THE END?

September 21, 2014, 4:00 PM: It's cold outside. The sky is the richest sapphire blue I've ever seen. There is a breeze blowing, and there is crispness in the air that welcomes the smell of fireplaces and hot chocolate. I close my eyes and take a deep breath that I hold for as long as I can. Standing in the driveway, I open my eyes and can see the leaves turning from green to brilliant orange, yellow, and red and are beginning to dot the landscape in a painting more beautiful than anything that has ever hung in an art gallery. It's been a busy day. A lot accomplished and still more to do. "What's the rest of today going to bring?" seems to be the primary question on my mind these days.

It's 4:00 AM. I am lying in my room listening to Stephen Curtis Chapman. Hovering halfway between sleep and sleeplessness, and I am aware that my door just opened.

My mother entered and softly said, "Come on, honey, your dad has passed."

Those seven words are something that will be burned into my mind for the rest of my life. I had thought about this moment for the last few years as my father's health declined. *How will I handle it when the time comes? My dad is my hero! I am going to lose my mind when he passes!* I thought to myself, yet I did not. Calmly I arose from my bed and went into my mother and father's room. This was the place that my father would spend the last seventy-two hours of his life. Pausing for a moment, I realized, as I took the twenty-seven steps from my room to his bedside, this would be the *last time* I would make this journey. I sat down beside my father and held his hand. Gone was the pain that my father had endured for the last several years. Gone was the suffering from being confined to a body that no longer wanted to cooperate. Gone was the uncertainty of what tomorrow would bring for my dad. What remained was a sense of peace—the likes of which I had never felt before. What remained was the vehicle that my father used for seventy-four years, but the essence or the "magic" that was my father was not in that room.

As I held my dad's hand and stroked his hair, I whispered these words, "You are free to fly now, Dad." The room was full of a comforting peace and a sense of correctness that I have never felt. I made the phone call to my brother, who was unable to get to Tennessee in time. I still have the record of that call: two minutes and twelve seconds made at 4:04 am. My heart went out to my brother who was desperately trying to get there in time.

I waited for the flood of emotions that would bring me to my knees! I waited for the uncontrollable "guttural" crying that I had heard so much about. I waited for the shortness of breath and the panic attack that I had anticipated for so many years prior as my father's health declined. None of those ever came. I went outside and looked into the dark sky. There were more stars out that early morning than could ever be counted.

In recent years, I had often wondered how I would respond to this moment in my life. Would I be angry at God for letting my father get sick? Would I yell and shout and swear at Him as I had done seven years earlier? Would I deny God? Blame God? Turn my back on God? No. I was reminded of a song that my father always loved called "God Wants to Hear You Sing." It is written by Rodney Griffin of the Southern Gospel trio Greater Vision. The words simply say

> God wants to hear you sing when the waves are crashing round you
>
> When the firey darts surround you and despair is all you see.

God wants to hear your voice when the wisest man has spoken and says your circumstance is as hopeless as can be…That's when God wants to hear you sing.

He loves to hear our praise on our cheerful days, when the pleasant times outweigh the bad, by far. But when suffering comes along

And we still sing Him songs, that is when we bless the Father's heart

—(R. Griffin, Greater Vision, *Perfect Candidate*, Daywind Records, 2000)

I raised my hands as high into the air as I possibly could and began to cry. Not in anger or hatred or in self-pity, but in gratitude. I began to thank God. I thanked Him for allowing me to have such an awesome man as my earthly father. I thanked God for not allowing my father to suffer too long. I thanked God for taking my father when He did. In the middle of my meeting with God, the song "See You in a Little While" by Steven Curtis Chapman began to play on my phone. I do not remember cueing this song or hitting Play. It must have been next in my playlist as I was listening to music only moments before. In my moment with God, I must have unknowingly hit the Play button on my phone. When I heard these words,

I hold your hand and watch as the sun slowly fades.

Far in the distance the Father is calling your name.

And it's time for you to go home and everything in me wants to hold on but I'm letting you go with this goodbye kiss and this promise…I'll see you in a little while

—(Steven Curtis Chapman,
The Glorious Unfolding,
Reunion Records, 2013)

I was overcome with gratitude and peace. A feeling of contentment overcame me and brought me to my knees. Kneeling in the middle of my parents' front yard at four in the morning, with my hands lifted high, the light of the phone in my left hand illuminating my immediate surroundings, my face toward the stars, crying and saying, "Thank you, God" over and over was the scene for the next fifteen minutes. It was a time of incredible closeness with my Heavenly Father while giving Him thanks for allowing me to have had the time with my Earthly Father that I had.

When I went inside, I observed my mother sitting at my father's bedside, and she was whispering words meant only for the ears of the man she had shared fifty years of her life. Her soul mate. She wiped his face softly and held his hand as we waited for the hospice nurse to arrive. The love this woman has for this man is at a level I can only hope to achieve one day.

Although the death of my father marked the end of his earthly journey, it sparked the beginning of a new chapter in the lives of those he left behind. He left a legacy that is more valuable than any trust fund or monetary inheritance. My dad set an example for all who knew him and loved him to follow. He had an effect on everyone he met. He had a profound effect on his family, and most of all, as far as I am concerned, his effect set the stage for my life.

A few hours later, the house was busy with activity. Hospice was there and was offering my mother and I counseling, should we need it. I stayed out of my mother and father's room to offer respect to my mother as she spent her final moments with my dad before the funeral home arrived. My heart was flooded with emotion as I witnessed her gentle nature in caring for my father as she waited for the time when he would have to go with the men who would soon come for him.

The doorbell rang. When I answered the door, I was greeted by two men wearing suits, who were very calm and gentle. Respect was evident as they spoke with my mother and I. My only concern was that I wanted them, and everyone who would come into contact with my father, to treat him with respect! I was assured that he would be, and I believed them in my heart. God was in that room that day.

I could feel Him there. As they left with my dad, I stood with my arm around my mother, supporting her and she supporting me. Seeing them drive out of sight was very difficult. I was reminded of the movies where the person is chasing after the car of a departing loved one. I found myself wanting to run after the car, but I knew that what had happened that morning was a release. It was a transition for my father from suffering to joy! From confinement to freedom! From life to *life*!

I turned to my mother and took a deep breath. She looked at me with the eyes of a woman who had just said good-bye to the man she loved for so many years, and she said, "I think I am going to go for a drive." She needed to be alone. During the time she was gone, I was busy restoring their bedroom, at her request, back to the way it used to be. Removing the hospital bed, oxygen machine, and other reminders of the sickness and suffering that had been so present in recent days.

When she returned, we sat in the kitchen and talked. Surprisingly we laughed about all the funny things that had occurred in the recent past and spoke of the joy and peace that Dad was experiencing at that very moment. It was at this time that I could feel emotions welling up inside. It was still not the typical emotions one would think you "should" experience at a time like this. It was emotions like gratitude and thankfulness that I was feeling very strongly.

Obviously I was emotionally destroyed because my hero, my father, had just passed away! But I was also feeling joy and gratefulness that God allowed me to have my dad as an example to live by for forty-seven years.

It was at the kitchen table that I told my mother about a conversation I had with God the night before. I had previously been in the room with my father and was watching him sleep. The rhythm of his breath in concert with the exhaust of the oxygen machine caused me to slip into a hypnotic trance for a while. At about 9:00 PM, I got up and went out into the garage and sat on his "Cadillac," which was his favorite mobility cart, and went for a drive around the yard. While I was slowly moving around the property, I was talking to God. I was thanking Him for all He had done in my life. I was thanking Him for my dad. I also asked God a simple question and made a request.

> "God, you know what's going on with Dad.
>
> You know his health and what he has been, and is, facing right now.
>
> God, if there is no hope of recovery and Dad is just going downhill, will you take him home now? Tonight?
>
> God, I know this is selfish of me, but I cannot help it.

You gave me a father who has always been strong physically, emotionally, and spiritually. He is growing weaker by the minute, and if he is on his way home, will you go ahead and take him home now?

Please don't let him linger like this for too long, God. Okay?"

I continued to pray as I was looking at the billions of stars in the sky. As I got to the driveway, after having ridden around the house a dozen times, I looked intently at the sky. There were more stars in the sky that night than I could remember seeing in a long time. I know this is going to sound like a cliché, but I don't care—frankly! It happened! As my eyes focused on all the points of light, I saw a shooting star! Most shooting stars last for only a second or two, but this one went from horizon to horizon! I didn't think too much of it other than *Wow! That lasted a long time!*

I went back inside and went into Mom and Dad's room. My mother had gone to bed and was sleeping in her bed next to Dad's hospital bed. I sat by Dad's side once again listening to him breathe in concert with the oxygen machine's exhaust. I decided to get my phone and record Dad's breathing as I had done so many times before with various conversations. I recorded exactly four minutes and thirty-seven seconds of his breath. Then I kissed him on the forehead, told him I loved him, and went to bed. Little did I know that those four minutes of recording would soon become more precious than gold.

I believe God honored my prayer that night. I believe that God was in the room with us and was waiting until I left the room so He could spend some time with my father. I believe that, during that time, set aside only for the two of them, God and my father decided it was time to go, at least physically. I *truly believe* that my father's spirit left his body earlier when I saw the shooting star. I know! "Come on, Guy! A shooting star? Really?" Yes, a shooting star! Really! I have only told a handful of people about the story of the shooting star. The simple reason that it sounds like a Hollywood movie script has prompted me to keep that moment very private! Until now.

My brother and his wife arrived later the morning of the twenty-second. I am choosing to leave the remainder of this story excluded, as at this point, it transitions into areas that are personal and private and include the emotions and feelings of others aside from myself. Suffice it to say that this time in our lives has brought us closer. It has built us up and has torn away at the walls built over a span of years. God moved in our lives on that day, as He has on so many days before. The difference on September 22 being that God proved beyond the shadow of a doubt, at least for me, that God is the Spirit of peace and comfort. That even during a time of emotional turmoil and physical loss of a hero, there can be "peace in the valley." I thank God for that day.

There is a movie that my dad loved to watch. It's called *City Slickers* (Castle Rock Entertainment, Nelson Entertainment, 1991) and stars Billy Crystal and Jack Palance. Dad used to cackle and laugh until he cried at that movie! In the movie, there are two memorable moments that apply to this book. One was when three of the main characters were asking each other, "What was the best and worst day(s) of your life so far?"

I would like to answer that question as though I was one of those actors sitting on horseback filming that scene. They would ask, "Guy, what was the worst day of your life?" I would answer,

> "September 22, 2014, because that is the day my dad died.
>
> That's the day that I lost my hero. That is the day that the man, who taught me all I know about how to survive in this world, passed away. That day was the day I lost my best friend.
>
> September 22, 2014, was the day that the man whom I could share anything with left me. I lost my father on September 22, 2014! That was my worst day!"

They would then ask, "Guy, tell us. What was your best day?" I would have absolutely no hesitation in my answer.

> "My best day would have to be September 22, 2014!
>
> Because on that day, God showed up! He showed me that He is in control of all things.
>
> God would reveal Himself to me in a way in which I could never possibly express.
>
> In the middle of what should have been a horrible tragedy, God gave me peace. God gave me comfort.
>
> My best day has to be September 22, 2014, because God parted my Red Sea.
>
> He showed me that He is absolutely real and that He has me in the palm of His hand."

There is another moment in that movie that has always stood out in my mind. It is a conversation between Billy Crystal's character and Jack Palance's character. Curly (Jack Palance) holds up his finger to Billy Crystal and says, "The meaning of life is this."

Billy Crystal says, "What? Your finger?"

Curly says, "No! The meaning of life is *one thing*!"

Billy Crystal says, "Oh…well, what's the one thing?"

Curly says, "That's what you have to figure out!"

What is the one thing that summarizes the meaning of your life? What is your one thing? I don't know about you, but the answer to that question was hard for me to narrow down! How can someone answer that question accurately? How can one possibly know what their "one thing" is? What could one thing that sums up the meaning of life possibly be? For me? It's the ARVIS Effect.

2

A IS FOR
ACCOUNTABILITY!

Dallas Texas, 1967. The hot Texas air is sweltering, and the ground cracks under the sun's intense stare. There is a bead of sweat forming on the brow of the man behind the wheel as the young couple and their two-year-old son head to the hospital! "He's coming!" they think to themselves as they speed toward the ER!

Sounds like a dramatic television show, doesn't it? Well, it's not. It's just my birthday.

Guy Michael Smith was born in mid May in the late 1960s to a young couple who were struggling to make ends meet and who were not afraid to work hard to provide for their young family. With their two-year-old son in tow, they welcomed their second son to the world. Born with a frown on my face and an attitude to match, I entered the world with a shout and the statement, "I am here, so ready or not, here I come!" Growing up in the late 60s, 70s, and 80s, I was fortunate to grow and mature in a time when the country still valued such things as family, honesty, and doing the right thing—even when no one's looking!

My earliest memory was when we were living in a small suburb of Dallas called Duncanville. My family rented a small farmhouse that was surrounded by cornfields, on three of the four sides, with the house backing up to what I thought was the haunted forest! My brother and I would have countless adventures in the cornfields as we would run from row to row having sword fights and playing cops and robbers! My dad worked hard as a plumber and a remodeling contractor and would spend most of the daylight hours earning money so he could support his family. My mother, who had the hardest job of all, would spend her time making sure my brother and I were safe as we jumped from tree to tree and from the hayloft of the barn, which had to have been a thousand feet off the ground! Or so I thought. From my perspective, we had a simple yet ideal life. My brother and I did not have to worry about strangers, immoral people, or being abducted! I know those things were happening at that time unfortunately, but my mother and father did a wonderful job of protecting us from such unimaginable things as these.

For as long as I can remember, my mother and father gave my brother and I responsibilities that were sometimes coupled with rewards! Sometimes not! Those responsibilities were called chores! Even though we did not have much, we had enough! We had food on the table, a roof over our heads, and those times were filled with laughter and plenty of adventure! I can remember being in prekindergarten, while we lived there, and we all had motorcycles. My brother and I had minibikes while my mother and father had full-size motorcycles. When my dad took time off on the weekends, we would sometimes go to the lake with our cousins and ride our minibikes and motorcycles all around the campground. Other times we would ride around in our own yard or the acres and acres of harvested fields that surrounded our property.

It was a simpler time back then. There was work, family, survival, and laughter! God was there the entire time. Even though my brother and I were too young to know much about God at that age, I know He was there. My mother was diligent in making sure we knew the stories of the Bible. The ways that God moves and works in our lives was taught to us at a very early age, thanks to my mother. It was during these sweet times of innocence that God revealed Himself in powerful ways.

As a young boy, I suffered from many problems with my ears and with my hearing. There were repeated visits to the doctor, tubes in my ears, and countless sleepless nights my mother spent at my bedside as I would cry under the pain of intense earaches. One evening, my mother scooped me up and took me to a church gathering where the evangelist Jimmy Swaggart was speaking. I was too young to remember the details of this encounter; however, I do remember this: Before we went, I could not hear; and after we left, I could hear everything! No more earaches, no more tubes! No more sleepless nights comforting a crying child.

Do I credit Jimmy Swaggart for my healing? Absolutely not. I credit my mother who had her faith firmly planted in the One who created me! She knew that with a "mustard seed of faith," she could move mountains! By her faith, she invited God to move a mountain in my life that night! God showed up!

As we grew older, my dad gave my brother and I the opportunity to learn a little about his profession. He was a plumbing superintendent at a small plumbing company in Texas, and he was able to take us to work quite often. We would learn things like inventory and how to do smaller, simple plumbing tasks; but being young kids, we would take every opportunity to sneak off and goof around. Although Dad was more tolerant than I would have most likely been, if it were me, he never missed the opportunity to teach us the value of *accountability*.

Even though I didn't realize it at the time, when my father would find us and make us return to work, he was teaching us the value of being accountable to someone aside from ourselves. He told us on many occasions:

> "I know it's fun to play around in the shop and to have fun.
>
> But I want you to remember that you are being paid to be here and to do a job. You are being trusted to do that job unsupervised, and you are expected to hold up your end of the deal, aren't you?"

Of course he was right. We would return to inventory, or whatever task he had us on, because we sure wanted that money at the end of the day! We had no idea that the money we were paid was actually coming out of my dad's own pocket! We were not on the company payroll like we thought! We were both under ten years old after all! But we thought that we were big-timers because we had a job and we got paid! My father was instrumental in teaching us that when we are at work, we are accountable to those we are working for! That those who own the company we are working for are accountable to the customer that hires them to do a job! That the customer is accountable to their family to make their situations better! My dad taught us that being accountable to someone else means far more than doing what we want to do.

"We have got to do something! He's getting left behind at school!" my mother said to my father one evening at the dinner table! The next morning, I was in the car with my mother, and she was taking me to school as she always did. This particular morning, the car, and my life, took a turn that I was not expecting. It was 1978, and I was halfway through my fifth-grade year in public school. I went to Jason B. Little Elementary in Arlington, Texas, and I was having a blast there! I was able to daydream, play, and goof around all day, and *I loved* it! I was doing great in school! In my opinion! In defense of the school, it was not necessarily their fault. The school was a new "open concept," which allowed me to watch other classes and daydream instead of being focused on what I was supposed to be doing. The school was overcrowded, and I simply began slipping through the cracks. My mother who was watching as my grades fell farther and farther took action. She was taking me to a new school!

Enter Pantego Christian Academy! PCA was a small private Christian school located across town from our house. We pulled up, and there were kids I did not know playing on a playground I was not familiar with surrounded by buildings I did not recognize! We went inside, and in the waiting room, I sat as my mom went into the main office for an interview. After what seemed like thirty-six hours later, the door opened and I was invited in. Shaking in my shoes, I stood up and walked the mile and a half (it seemed) from my chair to the door. I sat in the chair next to my mother and looked across the desk at what I thought was one of the most intimidating men I had ever seen. On the desk in front of him was a sign that said "Douglas Lesher—HEADMASTER." I *immediately* knew *who* I was about to be accountable to! Now of course, from my "little kid" point of view, and my fifth-grade mind, I was totally in over my head and he was going to be the taskmaster with the bullwhip! However, the truth of the matter was that I had just been introduced to one of two men at PCA that would help shape my youth and who would serve as examples to me for the rest of my life. Mr. Lesher (I still call him this to this day!) was actually one of the most caring individuals I would ever come into contact with. He would end up taking me under his wing and would reinforce the value of accountability that my mother and father instilled in me early on, and oh how he held me accountable!

After I was told that this was my new school, I was taken on a tour of the campus and introduced to many different teachers and administrators. Among those was a man named James (Jim) Rose. He was introduced to me as the PE Teacher and sports coach. I can remember looking at this man—who had big muscled arms, a ball cap perched on his head, and a whistle around his neck—as he looked back at me and said, "Well, hello, Mr. Smith," and he shook my hand with the grip of a two-ton vise! Needless to say, my world had changed instantly for the better on that day; although, at the time, I may have argued with you about that! Gone were the days of daydreaming and slipping by on excuses like "I don't know why I didn't do my homework!" or "I just do not remember being assigned that project!" Yes, that was a real excuse I tried once. Of course I did not realize that my life had changed for the better! To me, my life was *over*! I was in *prison*!

At PCA, I was held to a high standard of not only academic excellence but I was held accountable spiritually, physically, and morally as well! Being a Christian school, we began our day in prayer that was followed by a quick Bible study. Then it was on to academics! Really? *Where's the good time? How can I possibly goof off with only ten kids in my grade?* I thought. PCA was a very small school that had on average ten kids per grade. That's per *grade*, not class! It was very difficult to get by with anything! Thank God! There are many different stories I can share about my time at PCA. I will choose only two, as they clearly demonstrate the principle of accountability on which this chapter is based.

Well, into my time at PCA, I had become quite established in the school and quickly became comfortable with my friends, my status, and my popularity. Notice I failed to mention my studies. Jumping back to the early days, when I was first enrolled at PCA, I was given an IQ test. The reason for the test was that I was having such a hard time in public school, my mother and father were a bit concerned that I may have had a learning disability. If my mother were telling you this story, right about now she would squint her eyes and grit her teeth as she pointed her finger at you, as she said these words:

> "We were concerned that Guy had a learning disability because we would get reports from his teachers saying that our son is not a discipline problem in any way. He just cannot seem to focus, he daydreams and cannot seem to do the work.
>
> His father and I took him to have his IQ checked! It was then that we found out that his IQ was very high and that he was extremely capable, but he was just lazy! He was not interested in school! He did not have time for it!
>
> We could have strangled him!"

I could have told them that of course I was lazy! I wasn't being challenged in public school, and I was ten! As we fast-forward a few years, let me just say that "not being challenged" was no longer a problem! Mr. Lesher, who was in cahoots with my parents, decided to issue me a challenge. He said,

> "If you will actually do your homework *and* turn it in on time *and* get an A in the class each six weeks, we will pay you $10 per A on your report card!"

I thought, *Great! Are you kidding? I get paid for each A? This is awesome!* Then came the catch! He followed that statement with this:

> "However, if you fail to do your homework and turn it in *complete and on time*, you will get detention. If you get detention three times in one week, you will get three swats with the paddle from Mr. Rose, and they will not be comfortable!
>
> Likewise, you will not get paid for any grade short of an A on your report card!
>
> Do you accept?"

I thought about it for a minute and promptly accepted! Of course I could do this! I mean, after all, who in the world gets paid by the school to go to school? Me! That's who! Little did I know that the school was never paying me at all! I didn't realize that any money would be coming from my mother and father! Well, to make a long story short,

I believe, that year, I received somewhere in the range of seventy paddlings from Mr. Rose! Talk about being held accountable! I learned what accountability was for sure!

Why didn't I just turn in my homework? Why did I get sent to detention so many times? Simply stated, I had learned what accountability was for sure; however, I had not yet learned the value of it. Because I had parents that cared about me above all else, they sent me to a school that cared about the academic, spiritual, and moral growth of the kids under their care. Rare these days! My mother and father as well as Mr. Lesher and Mr. Rose, as well as a bunch of other teachers, were ensuring that one day something would "click" in my head and that someday I would "get it!" They were right!

Teachers like "Frau K," whose real name was Glenda Keilstrup. She was much more than my German teacher! She was also a mentor and an example for me. Plus, I was "in fifth-grade love" with her daughter Kristin! Six Flags Over Texas, Spee-Lunker's Cave! Ah, the memories!

The other story I would like to share basically deals with my interactions with Mr. Rose. I had been at PCA for a while when an opportunity to get involved with the drama class came up. Even though I was not much for being on stage (at that time), Mr. Rose needed someone to learn how to run the lights for the plays. He knew that I was the kid that always volunteered to fix the film projector and such, so he asked me if I would like to be the "lighting guy" for the school. I took to that like a duck to water. I jumped in with both feet. He saw a desire in me to learn, and he gave me the opportunity to do so. I quickly became the go-to guy anytime something technical needed to be done for the drama club—as well as the entire school for that matter. It was not until just a few years ago that I found out that Mr. Rose discovered that I had come to know far more about the school's lighting and sound systems than he did! Soon after he saw my eagerness to serve in that capacity, he asked me to take on other projects such as leveling the baseball field with a backhoe and helping rebuild the library when it was just a beat-up temporary building.

Unbeknownst to Mr. Rose, he set me on a path that would ultimately take me all over the world and would give me the opportunity to work with many celebrity performers and nationally known entertainers. His insight and opportunity, while I was in the sixth grade, would afford me a career that most people could only dream of. I will always owe Jim Rose a debt of gratitude for that!

I met some amazing people while I was at PCA. From Mr. Lesher and Mr. Rose to Mrs. Keilstrup, Mrs. Choun, Mr. McBride! All these people had a profound impact on my life! I also met some pretty amazing kids when I went to PCA. Starting in fifth grade and going through my freshman year in high school, I made some friendships that would last the rest of my life.

The point I am trying to make here is that I was fortunate enough, at a young age, to be taught the value of accountability by my mother and father, which was quickly reinforced by the staff at PCA. They all saw an opportunity to allow me to prove myself while holding me accountable at the same time! I am grateful for my time spent at this school and in the company of those who shaped my young mind and who gave me skills I would one day need to forge my own path.

Thank you for all you did for me, Pantego Christian Academy!

> Ac-count-abil-i-ty: An obligation or willingness to accept responsibility (or to account) for one's actions (*Webster's Dictionary* 2013)

Accountability is represented by the first latter in the ARVIS Effect. Accountability, today, means so much more than it did back in the good old days. Times have changed and so has the sheer number of people, places, and things that we are all accountable to in some regard. The choices we make and the choices made by one's parents, family, teachers, bosses, peers, or any other position of importance will have a profound impact on our accountability and will be firmly rooted in our psychology as we mature into adults.

All too often, however, we miss the most important point of all! What about accountability to ourselves? Or more importantly, to God? Being accountable to ourselves seems simple enough, doesn't it? But is it as simple as we think? I know, at least in my own life, it is often easier to do what feels right at the time than to do what we *know is right* and will stand the test of time. There is a huge difference! A clear example of this is a very personal story; I feel it's important to share it here as this story stands as clear testimony to the value of being accountable and the consequences of ignoring accountability.

Early in my career, as a lighting designer and audiovisual production company owner, I enjoyed tremendous success both financially as well as reward in status in the "who's who" of the production world. As so many before me will attest, "with great success comes many pitfalls!" That is true, my friends. I will be short and sweet here. At the pinnacle of my company's success, I was earning more money than anyone has a right to! We (my family) had everything one could hope for. I had it all! Cars, houses, boats, trips, status, friends, wife, kids, girlfriends—you name it! That's right, it's not a typo. I said wife, kids, and *girlfriends*!

Back in the early 90s and 2000s, my company was enjoying a wild ride. I was the twenty-something whiz kid of the audiovisual world. My company was contracted to one of the premiere resort hotels on the Gulf Coast of Florida. I was very young and very successful! At the same time, I was not accountable to anyone—including myself, my wife, and certainly not God! I was high on my own awesomeness, and I was not looking back. After a while, signs of trouble began to develop in my marriage, and rather than be accountable to each other, we fought and steadily drifted further apart. It takes multiple ingredients to bake a cake; likewise, it takes multiple players to end a marriage. I am only going to speak of the ingredients that I added to the mix as my actions were where my accountability fell short. Rather than focusing on what would stand the test of time, our marriage, I focused on what felt right at the time. I found an escape from my problems by making choices that would ultimately end a marriage and the vows that I took before God, but *who cares about God! What about my problems? Right?*

My relationship with God as an adult was not, at that time, what it is today. I will discuss this in great detail when we reach the *I* in the *ARVIS* Effect a few chapters from now. Suffice it to say "God and I were not on the same page" at this time in my life; therefore, I had no need to be accountable to Him, for sure—nor to anyone else for that matter! I do not bring up this time in my life lightly. I do not mention the end of my marriage to place blame on anyone other than myself. The point here is to illustrate the dangers of going through life and riding the wave of success in one area of our life while neglecting the accountability in all the other areas of our life.

Friends, accountability is one of the most important character traits that I can stress. As you have read, my father and mother had the insight to teach me the value of accountability at a very young age! They rooted it in my psychology early on. This is what makes my decision to ignore their teachings later in life that much more heartbreaking!

A lesson learned is trouble avoided.

—James Rose (1979)

Principle 1 of the ARVIS Effect: Accountability How to Live a Content and Fulfilled Life

Live every day being accountable for your statements and actions. Remember that there is always someone that you are accountable to. Whether you accept this fact or not is paramount to your contentment in life. No matter if it is your parents, wife, husband, children, boss, clients, customers, or anyone else. If you are a Christian, you are accountable to God first, yourself second, and the rest third. If you are not a Christian, you are accountable to yourself first and so on. Either way, we need to remember that life is not all about us. There are others out there whom we are accountable to that look to us for advice, assistance, companionship, friendship, and love. We are accountable for the things we say to these people, the things we tell ourselves, and the actions we take. Everything we do and say affects someone else for the better or worse. Being accountable to God and ourselves for the things we say and the actions we take serves as a mirror that reflects our true character.

3

R IS FOR RESPECT!

Pensacola, Florida. The beaches are sugar white and the water is a crystal-clear emerald green. The sun is shining brightly and the sea breeze is blowing just enough to take the edge off the heat generated by the sun. It's 1987 and it's June. The uniform rhythm of synchronized boots hitting the pavement echoes throughout the navy base. Pensacola Naval Air Station is the place. It's beautiful! Rich with hardwood trees, green grass, tradition, orders, and structure unique only to a military base. NAS *Pensacola: Naval Aviation Schools Command is the hub of naval aviation, and as a newly appointed survival instructor, it will serve as my home for the next several years.*

After graduating high school in 1985, I officially worked for my father, for a year or so, serving as one of his back-hoe operators. Being just eighteen, I was trusted by my dad with a brand-new company truck as well as a brand-new

Ford "Triple Nickel" 555 backhoe fresh from the factory. He and his business partner sent me all over the state of Texas (as well as other states) to work on various construction sites. My job was to "dig the rough," which meant to dig the ditches in the earth so the plumbers, who worked for my dad, could lay the pipe in the ground. As a young child, I had always exhibited interest in running the heavy equipment that my father's company had. As mentioned in chapter 2, I was proficient on the backhoe as early as age twelve. At age eighteen, I was good enough to run my own truck and had quickly become one of the most requested backhoe operators in my dad's company.

In doing my job, I had to be careful so that I did not destroy the forms erected by the concrete company, tear out the electrical lines placed by the electrical contractor, or rip out the gas lines installed by the gas company. There were a lot of obstacles that I had to negotiate as a respected backhoe operator. It was tough! One story would be told and retold by my father until the day he died.

> "We had to dig up a six-inch gas main that was buried ten feet deep below the sidewalk. All my backhoe operators were on other jobs, and the only one I had was my son. He was just eighteen and had never done anything this dangerous before. If he messed this up, he could cost the company $1,000

an hour to repair the gas line, and that's only if a spark doesn't kill everyone there first! I called him to the site, and he said he was ready for something like this. When he dug within a foot of the gas main, he started to dig at the speed of a crawl.

We were all nervous, but he wasn't. I was giving him play-by-play instructions when he looked at me and said, "Dad! I've got this. Trust me!"

He reached his bucket out as far as it would go, sunk the teeth into the dirt, and slowly pulled the dirt back, revealing the orange gas main snuggled directly between two of the teeth of the bucket!

The dirt fell out around the pipe and left it sitting on top of the ground.

He didn't leave a scratch on the pipe! My guys didn't even have to use a shovel!

It was the damnest thing I have ever seen!"

It was not until a few years later that I found out from some of the workers that the level of respect I gained from that job elevated exponentially that day. "Your dad was talking about that for years!" they said. I realized at that moment that, although I had always had the love of my father my entire life, I had earned my father's respect as well. Not simply by that job alone, but by being dependable—well, I wasn't dependable *all* the time! I was a teenager after all! And doing the best job I could in order to reflect well on my dad, his company, and myself. My father and I always enjoyed a great working relationship! Of course, he had his way and I had mine, but somehow, we always found the best way and had fun while doing it!

After having worked for my dad for a while after school, I decided I wanted to "start my real life" and decided to join the military. The US Navy to be specific! I joined in the summer of 1986 and was promptly shipped off to Great Lakes, Illinois (or Great Mistakes as we used to call it) for boot camp. It was July to be specific, and I was scared to death! *What had I done? Why are these people yelling so much? All they need to do is say what they want!* I had no clue what I was getting into, but I would soon learn!

> Re-spect: To feel admiration for (someone or something): To regard (someone or something) as being worthy of admiration because of good qualities (*Webster's Dictionary* 2013)

Because this chapter is about respect, I elected to share a little about my military career because there are no clearer examples of respect than the demands of the military. After going to boot camp and then "a" school in Lakehurst, New Jersey, I ultimately ended up in Pensacola, Florida.

I was a PR, or parachute rigger, which would eventually be renamed to ASE, or aircrew survival equipment man. Our primary duties were to pack the parachutes and service all of the survival equipment a pilot or a member of the aircrew would need in the case or ejection or other emergencies. Things like flares, weapons, LOX (liquid oxygen systems), ejection seats, parachutes, and other essential gear is what we were trained to handle on a daily basis. Upon graduation of "a" school, I ranked second in my class, which meant I got second choice of orders (orders are the instructions and paperwork that designate where you will be stationed next) out of a total of thirty! That was huge! When they spread out all the orders on the table in front of us, they said to take our pick according to class rank. When I looked at the orders, I saw Sea Duty, Sea Duty, Sea Duty, Sea Duty, Sea Duty, and on and on and on! Then I saw Shore Duty: NAS Pearl Harbor! And then I saw Instructor Duty: NAS Pensacola! Since I was number 2 in the class, I knew that I was either going to go to Hawaii or to Florida because I dang sure did not want to go on a ship if I didn't have to! The sailor who ranked number 1 picked Hawaii, so I was Florida-bound! I was going to be a survival instructor! Whatever that meant!

After a short Christmas leave, at home to see family and friends, I found myself at the doorstep of the Pensacola

Naval Air Station: Naval Aviation Schools Command. Hooyah! I was twenty years old and an instructor in the United States Navy! I had hit the big time of my life so far! I was assigned to a unit called DWEST (Deep Water Environment Survival Training), which was a division of Schools Command. Naval Aviation Schools Command was tasked with teaching anyone in naval aviation the skills needed to pilot, work in, or work on any naval aircraft. Our job in the survival division(s) were to equip and prepare any naval pilot or aircrew member how to survive if they either eject, bail out, or crash. If this took place over land, the student would attend LST (land survival training). If it took place over sea, they would go to DWEST.

As instructors, our jobs were to teach the students what they needed to know in order to survive in open water. We used tools such as parasailing, LRO (Life Raft Organization), zip lines, and classroom instruction. The students would come to us as a rotation in their total survival training schedule.

I've given you this background in my naval career in order to lay the foundation for the discussion about respect, which is the subject matter of this chapter. Anyone who knows anything about the military knows that respect is something that is demanded! Lower-ranking members must be respectful at all times of higher-ranking members. Higher-ranking members are "supposed" to be respectful of lower-ranking members, although this sometimes does not happen, unfortunately. Enlisted personnel are to show respect to officers by saluting them when their paths cross. Not doing this can result in disciplinary action against the offender. This brings me to an interesting story.

When I graduated "a" school and was designated an instructor, I technically outranked *any* student who came through our school. No matter their status as an officer or enlisted member of the military, I, as well as the other instructors, outranked them because instructors outranked students. Think about this for a moment. I was a rookie sailor who had just graduated boot camp a few months prior and I was placed in a position of authority over officers and enlisted who had been in the military for ten, twenty, or thirty years! There were high-ranking officers—from all branches of the military who were serving our country before I was even born—coming through my class. How is it possible that these distinguished men and women would have to show me respect? Yet they did!

When they were introduced as students to the instructors of the class, they were aware that they had to call us sir and to salute us as they would any member of the military who outranked them. Now of course, as an "e-nothing" as referred to myself, I never even thought about abusing such an obvious shift in power! As the next story will illustrate. However, I mention this part of my experience to show that respect is not awarded, it is earned. Those pilots, aircrew, and other distinguished members of our fighting forces earned my respect through their time in service, the experience they had, and the rank they had achieved. Likewise, they respected me because even though I had not been in the military as long as they had been, nor had I accomplished the things they had, they knew that I would not have been an instructor in the US Navy had I not earned my place by being the best I could have possibly been when I was being trained.

After having been in Pensacola for some time, I became familiar with the system and figured out ways to ally myself with the right people that could help me along my path. One of those people was a drill instructor who was assigned to instruct the Aviation Officer Candidates (the boot camp for anyone who wants to be a pilot or navigator in the US Navy). I had become a bus driver for the "poopies" (they were called this because their barracks smelled like…well…you catch the drift) and would transport them wherever they needed to go. During the time the students were in class, the drill instructor and I would sit in the bus and talk.

Given that most drill instructors in the military are enlisted, and in this particular case, he was the DI (drill instructor) for candidates who would eventually graduate boot camp and would instantly outrank him by becoming an officer, I asked him if he had ever had a situation where an officer candidate graduated boot camp as an 01 (lowest rank in the officer core but still outranks the highest rank in the enlisted core) and then sought him out to "put him in his place"? He sat back and told me of one ensign (Naval 01) that had graduated boot camp at 9:00 AM. Then at 10:30, the newly commissioned ensign was walking down the street with his family who had come for his graduation. The ensign saw my drill instructor friend walking on the opposite side of the street. The DI told me that he could tell that the ensign wanted to show off in front of his family and was going to make the DI drop (do push-ups). The DI said the ensign approached with his girlfriend on his arm, and when he did, the DI saluted him. The ensign said,

> "Boy, the shoe's on the other foot now, son! For sixteen weeks, you 'dropped' me, yelled at me, and made me sweat! It's your turn now, boy! DROP!
> And give me one hundred!"

With my jaw on the floor, I asked the DI, "What did you do?"

He said, "I dropped! If I hadn't, I would have been disobeying an officer and would not be showing him the respect the uniform and rank carries!"

I said, "WHAT! SHOWING HIM RESPECT?" I then said, "He is in no way showing you respect! He's is mocking you and taunting you simply because he now outranked you!" Little did I know I was about to learn the value of respect in the next statement! The DI turned to me and said these words:

> "Had I not complied with the ensign's request, I would be disrespecting the oath I took to uphold the traditions of the US Navy. Even though I was well aware that he was showing off for his family, I would have been in the wrong had I refused his order. As it happened, the CO (commanding officer) of the boot camp happened to be looking out his office window when this took place. He saw the whole thing. As I was on push-up number 60, I heard the CO's voice over the yells of the ensign. The CO gave me an order to stop doing push-ups and to stand to my feet. He then looked at the ensign and removed the brand-new shoulder boards he had just been awarded. Removed the single gold bar on his uniform collar and said, 'Son you are now officially *out* of the US Navy. You just lost the commission you worked so hard for because you obviously did not learn the meaning of the word *respect*!'"

This man who had just spent the last sixteen weeks of his life in an intensive training program learning to become an officer in the US Navy just lost it all because he did not show respect, which had been drilled into him at every turn of his training.

There are many stories that I could share about respect and my military career. Suffice it to say, this one drives the point home pretty clearly.

Earlier in my professional life, while I was working for my dad, I was sitting on the backhoe and had dug a deep ditch in the rain. There was a deadline, and the job had to be finished that day. The Texas sky had opened up, and it came a "frog strangler," as my father used to say! I had opened the ditch, and we were all down in the ditch struggling to get the pipes mated together. Soaked and covered in mud, we were miserable! I saw my father's truck pull up to the jobsite. He was in the driver's seat, and I could tell that he had just come from a meeting because he was wearing a white dress shirt and a tie! If you knew my dad, you also knew that Dad did not usually dress in a suit! So wherever he was coming from, it must have been important.

When he realized that we were having such difficulty with finishing the job, he jumped out of his truck and came to the ditch. With dress shirt, tie, dress pants, and shoes on, my dad jumped down in that ditch; and with his help, we got the pipes mated together! We accomplished the job because my dad knew the value of never asking someone to do something that you won't do yourself! He totally trashed his expensive shirt, shoes, pants, and all. Why did he do that?

My father taught me through observing him how to earn the respect of others. By not sitting in his truck, nice and dry, and simply calling in someone else to help—he jumped in there and demonstrated respect for his men by not asking them to do something that he wouldn't do himself. The men that worked for my father would have walked through fire for him! They knew that "Smitty" never forgot where he came from. They knew that they could count on Smitty to do the right thing. They respected him through and through.

It's through the examples that I shared above that I learned the value of respect. Whether it's respecting others or having respect for ourselves, respect is one of the foundations by which we build and maintain relationships. If you cannot be respected, you likely cannot be trusted. Like the DI in the Navy or my father in the mud and rain, respect is earned, not bestowed. Sure, in the military you have to show respect at all times, but to me, that kind of respect is not true respect. It's simply military courtesy. True respect is the belief that a person is worthy of trust, through the trials of fire and the test of time. Simply demanding respect is not enough. You have to work for it! We all know that people do not value things when given to them as much as when they have to work for it! Work for respect! Earn it! It's well worth the effort!

Principle 2 of the ARVIS Effect: Respect
How to Live a Life Full of Respect
toward Others as Well as Ourselves

Respect for yourself and for others is one of the main keys to success in life. Without respect, we really have little to build on. Respect for oneself begins by looking in the mirror and being content with what you see. (Notice I said "*content* with what you see" and not "*happy* with what you see"!) I am not talking about the physical reflection, mind you. To some degree, we are all working with what God gave us, so to be unhappy with the unchangeable aspects of your physical reflection is to be unhappy with the reason it gets hot in the summer! We cannot control that! I am referring to what you see when you look deep into your own eyes. Do you see someone that stands by their word? Do you see an honest person or a liar? Is the person in the mirror selfish or selfless? Is the person in the mirror a giver or a taker? Taking a good, long, and honest look at ourselves in the mirror and asking ourselves the hard questions can reveal a lot about who we really are. If you are ashamed of some of the answers to those questions, it's okay! We all have things we need to work on. The question is, are you going to keep on doing the same things while expecting different results? Or are you going to try a new approach? Are you going to try and do it alone? Or are you going to ask God for His opinion and guidance? All too often you hear people in the media say "so and so disrespected me and I am not going to tolerate being disrespected!" They are all puffed up and are going to show the world that they are someone who won't be "disrespected." Rather than take that approach, why not ask ourselves, "What am I able to change that will make me a better example of the way God wants me to be?" Instead of using the old phrase "WWJD?" ("What would Jesus do?"), try using this one instead: HWJDI? or "How would Jesus do it?" The *what* is easy. The *how* is the hard part. Seek God. Ask Him. He will let you know what to do.

4

V IS FOR VIGILANCE!

Beams of light are moving through the evening air, cutting a path through the air, as the beat of the music causes the crowd to dance. Conversations are had on this moonlit evening by the ocean. There is a light breeze as the crowd is celebrating the accomplishments of the corporate team. The chefs are carving at the different serving stations, and the bartenders are pouring their unique specialties. Social energy pulses as the main event of the convention draws near. In the distance, out of the view of the crowd, technicians hurry to ready themselves for their big debut. Tensions are high, voices are low, and the seriousness of what is about to take place is palpable.

While I was growing up and maturing under the guidance of my mother and father, as well as the countless number of mentors and teachers that would enter and exit my life, one thing that always remained constant was my parents' willingness to let me try new things. As I stated previously, at the ripe age of eighteen, I had become quite good as a backhoe operator in my father's company.

Often there were other companies, on the same jobsite, that had their own backhoe operators, who I had come to know. One afternoon I found myself working in Fort Worth on a large warehouse construction project. My father's company had been hired to install the plumbing and gas lines for this major construction site. As usual, I was on my backhoe digging when I noticed a familiar truck and tractor rig pull on-site. *Hey, it's Ray!* I thought. Ray was a backhoe operator for a local utility contractor and was very good at what he did! In the "backhoe circles" (if there is such a thing), he was known as being the best of the best. His ditches were the straightest, the prettiest, and the most uniform. He was *fast* too! I know…thrilling, right? We're talking about digging ditches, Guy! Come on! Read on. There is a reason for this story!

When Ray got on-site and began his work, he had to dig in about the same location as I. We said our greetings; then he went to work. Shortly, the men on Ray's crew were down in the hole, which was actually a sewer main, doing their thing. I could not see what they were doing because I had my own ditch to dig! And, man, was my ditch straight and pretty! The best of the best, the top gun of backhoe operators was right next to me and could see everything I was doing! I had to be on my A game!

Things were going along smoothly for both crews until suddenly I heard a loud commotion from Ray's crew in the sewer main. There was yelling and screaming, and as I watched Ray jump from his backhoe and run to the ditch, I discovered that his men were in trouble. To make a long story short, three of Ray's men died that day. The methane gas that builds up in any sewer line is toxic! When a person is going to be exposed to methane gas for any length of time (especially when it's concentrated in a sewer main), you must wear a respirator. Ray's men knew this. However, they were in a hurry, and they thought that they could just "get in and get out!" They were wrong.

As they were working in the hole, one man had to venture farther into the sewer main in order to repair a broken seal. He should have only been gone for a minute or two; however, when he had not returned after ten minutes, another crew member went to look for him. That crew member never returned either. Then a third went to check, never to return. As panic set in, the crew feared what was already tugging at the back of their minds. The rest of the crew ran to their trucks to get their respirators and ventured deep into the sewer. To their horror, they found all three crew members had succumbed to the methane gas as one crew member tried to pull the previous crew member to safety. That was a sad day in the construction world in Texas.

The point of this story is vigilance, or the lack of it. Even though the experienced crew knew the proper procedures to follow, they were not vigilant in watching out for dangers—either hidden (like methane gas) or evident. Their experience, in this case, worked against them. They thought they could cheat the system. However, the system cheated them out of their lives that hot summer day.

Upon hearing this news, my father called a company-wide meeting. We discussed what had happened on the jobsite that day. Even though the accident had not happened to anyone in my dad's company, he took it personal, just as though it had. "If anyone is caught doing anything like that in this company, you will be let go on the spot!" Dad said. He was not angry, he was scared. Scared because the accident on Ray's crew could easily have been prevented. My father was vigilant in making sure that safety protocols were followed and that his crew knew what to do and how to do it.

Standing on a barge that was floating in the bay near Sandestin Beach Resort in Destin, Florida, I was doing what I always did! Designing a show for one of our clients.

This year I was executing a light show coordinated with a live fireworks show for one of our huge annual convention guests. This company held its annual meeting on our resort, and every year, I was tasked with one-upping myself from the show I produced the year before. Each year, the convention coordinators said, "What are you going to do for us this year, Guy?" I knew that those statements were meant as a challenge to be bigger, more exciting, and more impressive than the year(s) prior.

This year, I was recalling everything I had ever known about putting on a show! We had all of our moving lights (the lights you see at a concert that move around and change colors and patterns), trusses, lasers, video projection gear, screens, sound, and special effects on-site. All day had been spent running wire, making thousands of connections, and running tests in the heat of the Florida sun. This year's show was going to include a water-launched fireworks show that would be timed and coordinated with the custom-made soundtrack and light/laser show as well as close-proximity fireworks launched from the pool deck area. This was huge! Nothing like this had even been attempted at our little resort before. The hours went by, and the crew was working hard to ensure that each of their areas of responsibility were complete on time. Personally, I was traveling around the show site checking on each crew member and offering assistance when they hit an obstacle. I soon found myself on the launch barge helping my explosives team wire the show. I must go into a bit of detail here as it will help build an understanding of the importance of vigilance when in this line of work.

A community-size fireworks display consists of far more than one can buy at a local fireworks supply store. Federal permits must be obtained. Special transportation must be arranged because you are, in essence, hauling bombs. When handling these "shells," the crew must take great care in making sure that there are no static electricity charges around as well as open flame or sparks. Special launch tubes, made of high-density abs plastic, are erected.

Each firework or "explosion" that the audience sees originates in the shell, or a cannonball-looking device that is usually round and wrapped in plain brown paper. There is a three-foot "quick burn" fuse coming out of the top of each shell. A "lift charge" is seated under each shell, which makes it appear that the cannonball is sitting on top of a small cup. When the fuse is lit, it rapidly ignites the lift charge that shoots the shell out of the launch tube to the desired elevation. Shells are measured in inches. A three-inch diameter will travel three hundred feet in the air. Four inches to four hundred feet and so on. This show used shells from four to eight inches in diameter. Once the shell is launched into the air, the explosion of the launch ignites a "timed" fuse that burns upward along the outside of the cannonball-looking shell. When it reaches the inside of the shell, it explodes in the brilliant display that everyone on the ground sees! Depending on the desired look, there are also "minicharges" in the center of the main shell that are ignited when the main shell explodes. This results in the brilliant visual flash in the sky followed by a secondary visual look a few seconds later.

Now, on with the story.

About an hour until showtime, everything was complete. All the connections were made. Tests complete. Communications were up, and we were ready to go. The only thing left to do was to reconnect the master control line, which was approximately one thousand feet long and stretched from the shoreline, behind the pool deck, out into the water to our control boat. The control boat had its own control line that extended another five hundred feet to the launch barge. All these connections had been made and tested prior, but were disconnected prior to showtime to ensure that there was no possibility of an accidental signal, which could start the show prematurely.

"Fifteen minutes!" I communicated to my team(s) on radio. From the control boat, I could see the crowd dancing and having a great time. Our lights were going and the band was great! "This is going to be the biggest show so far!" said one of my crew members. "Let's stay focused," I said.

One of the most important jobs in a show like this is crowd control. Usually we are talking about the crowd on land in the areas immediately surrounding the launch site. This time, however, we had to deal with crowds on the water! Our activities that day had resulted in a gathering of boats that we had not counted on. Curious onlookers, wanting to know what was going on, became a serious problem the closer showtime came.

We had contacted the Florida State Marine Patrol, which was onsite and was doing a good job at keeping the one thousand feet "safe zone" around the launch barge.

"Five minutes," I said to the crew. "Prepare the barge," was the next command. This was the signal for the launch crew to arm the circuits that would split off to all the launch tubes preparing them to be fired. Once the system was armed, the launch crew got into their boat and sped away from the barge toward our control boat. All systems were ready! "Arm the master control line," which was the line extending from the shore to the control boat. The MCL (master control line) was reconnected, and we got "green lights" across the board. All systems were armed and ready! We now had a barge that was loaded with over five hundred "bombs" that were ranging between three to eight inches in diameter. This was serious business.

"Thirty seconds. Ten. Nine. Eight. Seven. Six. Five. Four. Three. Two. One. Go!" The music rang out, and the lights began to move in concert with the music. The screens went from random images to the coordinated video that had been shot of the groups' convention. The lasers shot out over the audience's heads, and the crowd cheered! They clapped with delight as they saw the faces of their friends and colleagues on the two massive video screens! The Marine Patrol was guarding our "safe zone" like it was the front line in a major battle. There were hundreds of boats in the harbor waiting to see what was about to happen. "One minute!" I said. Which was code for "one minute to launch."

Exactly two minutes and twenty-eight seconds into the final show of the convention, the go command was given from the control boat. The barge erupted in a brilliant flash of light as the individual shells were given their commands to launch! Each firing in a predetermined time! Flying hundreds of feet in the air and exploding in a brilliant display of color! Each second, dozens of launch tubes rang out with the explosions of the "lift charges" as they were propelled to eight hundred feet in the air! The music was perfectly timed with the explosions, and the lights changed color to match the brilliant hues exploding all around us. It was beautiful! The noise was deafening as the eight-inch shells fired. The crowd went wild!

The finale came, and the barge came alive with hundreds of explosions in thirty seconds. The echo of the fireworks display was heard five miles away as the water reflected the sound like glass. The show was coming to an end as the final shell was launched. It exploded five hundred feet in the air into the shape of the company's initials! It was a custom shell that I had requested to be made as the "icing on the cake!" And it worked! This show was a huge success and was the largest show of its kind on the Gulf Coast of Florida at the time.

Why did I share this story as part of this book? I am sure some of the readers will be thinking, "Where is the tragedy? I thought there was going to be an accident or something?" No. No tragedy. No accident. Why?

As my father taught me all my life, being vigilant, guarding against danger, being thorough in everything is the only way to avoid accidents like the one Ray's crew experienced that day in Texas. As an owner of a production company that was responsible for the lives and well-being of over thirty technicians, as well as three hundred guests on the day of that show, it was totally in my interest to be vigilant!

Someone could have easily lost a limb, an eye, or even their life that day on the water. Being vigilant in protecting the public safety and the safety of my crew was paramount in my mind. There was far more time spent on ensuring the quality of the equipment and that safety procedures were followed than was spent on the show itself. All in all, we worked for fifteen hours on a show that would last less than fifteen minutes!

How often have you read about someone not being vigilant and ending up in the hospital? Perhaps it has happened to you? The famous last words "Watch this!" ring true in thousands of injuries and deaths in America each year.

What about being vigilant in other areas? Areas that do not come to the forefront of our minds when thinking about avoiding danger? What about being vigilant in our marriage? Guarding against dangers like the temptation to stray when the "going gets tough"? How about being vigilant about how we speak to our loved ones when we are angry? Or being vigilant in our relationships to ensure against the danger of stagnation and complacency?

> Vig-i-lance: The quality or state of being wakeful and alert: degree of wakefulness or responsiveness to stimuli (*Webster's Dictionary* 2013)

Being vigilant goes far deeper and is far more important than making sure you do not get hurt physically. What about emotional vigilance? What about spiritual vigilance? Being vigilant in guarding your emotions does not mean being "guarded" with those you love. It means being open with the ones you love. All too often we tend to "clam up" or "shut down" when it comes to our emotional lives. Being open with our emotions and letting them out is paramount to emotional health. "Wearing your heart on your sleeve" is not a bad thing when you need to express what's going on inside. Being too sensitive or taking things personally when they are not intended to be personal are a result of poor communication, which is a result of not being vigilant in our emotional life.

Communicating openly and freely is vital! I cannot stress that enough! If you have something to say, *say it*! However, remember that part of being vigilant in our emotional life is remembering that others have emotional lives as well. Being vigilant in our emotions also means being vigilant in the emotional lives of others in guarding against being harsh or brash when trying to communicate with others. I am guilty of this quite often! I have a point to make or an issue to express, and sometimes in my presentation of those points or issues, I can come across as "harsh" or "in your face." I certainly do not intend to come across that way, but sometimes I do. I own it. Thankfully, I enjoy relationships with people that will not hesitate to tell me, "I get your point, but don't be an—about it!" Then, I am reminded that I may have not been as vigilant in my communication style as I might have thought.

What about in our spiritual lives? Is vigilance an issue here? You bet it is! Safeguarding our spirituality is one of, if not the most, important thing in this book. The Bible says,

Be of sober spirit, be on the alert. Your adversary, the devil, prowls around like a roaring lion, seeking someone to devour. But resist him, firm in your faith, knowing that the same experiences of suffering are being accomplished by your brethren who are in the world. After you have suffered for a little while, the God of all grace, who called you to His eternal glory in Christ, will Himself perfect, confirm, strengthen and establish you. (1 Peter 5:8–10, NAS)

Think about this verse for a moment: "Your adversary, the devil, prowls around like a roaring lion, seeking someone to devour." Here we have a clear description of the biggest reason to be vigilant.

Think about a lion on the African Savannah for a moment. What have you seen on TV? You see these big majestic cats lying around under a shade tree grooming themselves, right? Then we will see them on the hunt running full speed after their prey. When they catch their prey, they let out a thunderous roar informing other animals to stay away. Think about the prey for a moment. Do you think it got caught by the lion because it was on its guard? Do you think the prey was being vigilant and watching for danger when the lion attacked? No. Its guard was down. It surveyed the area looking for danger and did not see any clear signs of danger. It shifted its eyes for a moment, and that is when the lion, which was hiding in the shadows, attacked!

The same thing happens to us. We are taught to look for danger, and we do! We govern what we watch on television, the music we listen to, the movies we go see. We are vigilant! Until we get comfortable. That is when the lion strikes! Be always mindful of the things that we allow into our lives and the lives of our families. Do not get too comfortable by swimming with the crowd. Be vigilant! Be aware. This does not mean that we should live in *fear*! God is not the spirit of fear! We should, however, seek God first in our decisions. Let them become His problem to deal with, not ours. I promise you He can handle whatever you may be going through!

Principle 3 of the ARVIS Effect: Vigilance How to Live a Life while Being Mindful of Who We Really Are

> Watch over your heart with all diligence, for from it flow the springs of life. (Proverbs 4:23, NAS)

This is one of the most important scriptures in the Bible, in my opinion. It illustrates the importance of safeguarding not only what is allowed into our hearts, but what comes out as well.

This chapter has talked continuously about the importance of being vigilant or safeguarding ourselves against danger. My mother and father taught us that physical danger is scary enough, but what about spiritual danger? Dangers of the spirit are much harder to recognize than a lion hiding in the bushes. My parents taught me early on that the greatest threat to our spirituality is complacency. Becoming too comfortable with ourselves is a quick way to end up in trouble. I've seen this firsthand! As Christians, we should be ever mindful of the exposures we allow ourselves to absorb.

I am reminded of the story about the Boiling Frog.

> If you take a frog and place it into a pot of boiling water, what will he do? He will jump right out and hop away. However, if you take the same frog and put him in a pot of cold water, he will just sit there and swim around. If you slowly turn up the heat until the water starts to boil, he will stay in the pot and slowly boil to death. Why? Because he has become comfortable with his environment. As his environment slowly began to change around him, the frog never noticed. By the time he notices, it's too late!

Sound familiar? Violence on TV? Sex on TV? Infidelity being spun as acceptable? Drugs to speed us up? Drugs to slow us down. Drugs to make us happy! Drugs for anything we wish! It's our right! Right? Turn to any news channel at any time of the day and try to find something being reported that is good! You won't find it…Well, you may, but it will be buried in the middle of all of the death and destruction that make the headlines.

The exact same thing happens to us. When we first became Christians, we were keenly aware of any hot water that may have awaited us. However, over time, we become desensitized to things like violence on TV, declining social abilities due to ever-increasing cell phone usage, and other socially accepted trends that we would have never stood for years ago. Convenience has replaced substance. We must be vigilant to safeguard against complacency in our own life before we can guard against danger in the lives of our family. Don't get complacent. The reward is worth it!

5

I Is for Inspiration!

Los Angeles, California, in the month of May. The plane lands, and a man with a sign is standing at the gate. It's 2007, and it has been a good year so far. Business is good, and all is well in the universe! A short ride to what would appear to be the "ghetto" would stop at a large "professional"-looking building. A sign that had been "tagged" with graffiti read, "The House Ear Institute." A long walk from the parking lot would end up in the busy lobby of one of the most premier health clinics in the world. A greeting from the doctor would be followed by the reading of an MRI. "You have a large tumor growing on the nerve that connects your right ear to your brainstem. It has to come out. This is serious, and things do not look promising, so you should get your affairs in order." The world stopped spinning. Life was hanging in the balance.

In Texas, the summertime is hot and dry. My father was working hard to provide for his family, and life as a plumber was tough! The hot sun would relentlessly beat down zapping every ounce of strength he had. Still he forged on. Through the years, my father became more and more knowledgeable in his field and therefore took on more responsibility. "We really depend on Smitty," said one of his bosses. "We know that when Smitty is on the job, everything will be done right!" This was the sentiment of the company Dad worked for.

My father was not "all business and no play" though. He loved to have a good time and believed that it was possible to have fun while working yet still do the best job he could. My father loved to be the practical joker and would pull little pranks here and there to lighten the mood on a hot Texas day. Even though Dad was the laughter that would fill a room, he was not much for having pranks pulled on him! My father had a reputation for being a little bit jumpy. Well…a lot jumpy to be totally honest. It was quickly learned by all that you did not sneak up on Smitty because in startling him, he may reactively hit you! Not intentionally of course; it would just be a "fight or flight" reaction. This was a well-known fact around the shop, so the men devised ways to pull a prank on my father where they would not have to be around.

One morning, the men gathered in the shop and decided that they wanted to play a joke on my father. They had found a rat that had been caught in a trap the night before. They took the rat and placed it above the sun visor in my dad's work truck. When my father arrived, it was business as usual. "Shop meeting at seven, guys!" my father would say. The coffee was already brewed, and the sweet smell permeated the entire building. On any given day, there may or may not be a box of donuts on the table as the men gathered to get the plan for the day. They were all standing in a semicircle as my father gave them their assignments. Smirks appeared on the faces of a few men as they knew what would happen shortly after the meeting adjourned.

"Okay! Let's hit it!" my father said as the men scattered to their particular areas. Little did my father know that they were all accumulating by the window so they could see him as he drove off. They all knew that my father's habit was to leave the shop and turn east (facing the morning sun). They saw his truck pull up to the street. Right turn signal goes on! Then the shiny red brake lights dim as he pulls out onto the street. About thirty seconds after turning on to the street, the men see my dad's truck weaving, and suddenly the truck stops, and my dad's door opens as he flies out of the truck! He had obviously lowered his sun visor, revealing the rat as it fell into his lap! Surprisingly my father had a great sense of humor about the prank even though the men "scattered" and no one claimed to be the mastermind.

You might be thinking, "What a cruel joke! He could have gotten seriously injured! Or had an accident!" Well, true. However, it just so happened that my dad's place of employment was situated on a road that was not that busy during the early morning hours. However, in the interest of public safety, this is not a prank that I would recommend.

After many years at this place of employment and after having climbed the ladder of responsibility, my father found himself wanting more from his professional life than his current employment could offer. He had been remodeling houses on the side and was making decidedly more money remodeling houses than he was at his full-time job. After numerous conversations with my mother, family, and friends, he decided to strike out on his own. Not knowing what the future would hold, my father set his sights on creating a successful business of his own.

He gave notice, and that was it. Not knowing what the precise next step should be, he just did what he knew, did the best job he could for the remodel jobs he currently had. As word of Smitty's departure spread, it caught the attention of one of my dad's former bosses. Knowing the knowledge my dad had as well as his ability to identify and inspire the crew, this boss sought my father out and proposed to become partners in a new plumbing corporation. The rest is plumbing history.

S&S Mechanical Contractors Inc. would soon become one of the largest and most well-respected mechanical contracting companies in the Dallas—Fort Worth area during the late 70s and 80s. With hundreds of employees and trucks along with jobs all over the country, my dad and the company he formed served as an inspiration to me from as early as I can remember. With no guaranty of any future, my father took a risk and stepped out of his comfort zone and tried something that was considered by many to be foolish. "You are going to leave a steady paycheck to start your own business? You're crazy!" was the popular opinion of his decision.

My father's inspiration would serve as my inspiration for most of my professional life. Anyone who knows me knows that I have never been afraid to swim against the current or to try new things, even when it may be against popular opinion. "Nothing ventured, nothing gained" was the model that I learned to live by through the example from my dad.

As a former employee of mine once said, while describing a potentially risky move my own company was going to make, "There is safety and comfort in being secure. However, the true reward is shrouded in the risks we take" (Ron Draper 1999).

In early 2006, while I was working as the technical director for the Miracle Theater in Pigeon Forge, Tennessee, I started to experience numbness in my lower right jaw. I attributed it to poor dental work or perhaps stress. As time progressed, so did the numbness as it grew from my lower jaw to encompass the entire right side of my face. Feeling a distinct line between sensation and numbness—which ran down the middle of my forehead, nose, lips, and jaw—my face was divided into two different halves. I decided to quit acting like it was not happening and went to the doctor. "Well, it's probably inflammation of the trigeminal nerve," the doctor said. "There is a remote possibility that it could be something else, but that is so rare I hate to even mention it," she continued. "There is a very rare brain tumor called an acoustic neuroma, which could produce the same symptoms, but I would doubt that would be your situation. To be certain, I would like to send you for an MRI, okay?"

A few days later, I found myself in a hospital gown lying on a small table that slid my head into a giant metal circle. "Hold very still," a voice said through the speaker above me. I was as still as I could possibly be as I stared at the mirror that allowed me to see my feet, control room, and the area surrounding my immediate location. *Bam bam bam bam bam!* was the sound coming from somewhere deep inside the machine. The MRI machine was bombarding my head with a very strong magnetic field that resulted in a very clear image of the inside of my head. I felt someone touch my leg, and I began to slide out of the machine. "You can get dressed now, then wait here," they said. I did so, and just sat waiting for them to return.

Soon the technician, who had been helping me, entered the room and handed me a DVD disc.

He said, "Here, keep this for your records."

I said, "What is it?"

He said, "It's a copy of everything the doctor is going to look at. He's out of town at the moment, so it will be a few weeks before he can read the results."

I said, "What did you see?"

He said, "I am not qualified to read the images. You will have to wait for the doc."

With disc in hand, I went home.

After having been home for a few hours, I remembered the disc. I took it out and put it into my computer's disc drive. There were a lot of files on the disc that I did not recognize, but there was one that ended with .exe. I knew that this was an executable file, so I clicked on it. My computer promptly responded by installing a program on my hard drive, and after a few seconds, a set of instructions popped up. "Click here and scroll down to view images," it said. So I did. As the images flipped one to another, much like an old flip animation book I would make as a kid, the images of the inside of my head started to unfold. Starting at the top of my head and working their way down, I could see the top of my skull, then the top of my brain. *This is cool*, I thought as I scrolled further and further down into my brain. *There are my eyes! My optic nerve!* It was very cool to see the inside of my head! *There are my sinus cavities and my—hello! What in the world is that?* At that moment, I was deep enough into my brain that I could see my ears. On the left side was the same kind of light and dark gray images I had seen prior. On the right side was a large white walnut-shaped image. The deeper I scrolled and the bigger it got, the deeper my heart sank.

I saved a copy of it and sent it to my brother who is a speech pathologist at MD Anderson Cancer hospital in Houston, Texas. "Oh man! Who is that?" he asked. "It's me," I said. Silence on the other end of the phone. "I'll call you back," he said softly into the phone and hung up. At the same time, I uploaded my image to Google and did a reverse image search that yielded one result: acoustic neuroma. My world shattered, and the earth stopped spinning. *I not only have a brain tumor, I have a* very rare brain tumor*! Oh my god!*

The phone rang, and my brother said, "I've shown your image to a few of my neurosurgeon friends, and they have all said you have an—"

"Acoustic neuroma?" I said.

"Yes, how did you know?" he asked.

"Google!" I said.

We then began to formulate a plan. Who to see, what to do. My mind darted from taking action to ending my life on my own terms. From fighting to giving in. From anger to *rage*! *How could you do this to me, God! Have I not done what you wanted?* Those were just two of the questions I screamed at God while cursing Him in my front yard. Just as Jacob wrestled with God in the book of Genesis, I decided to "take on God" in my front yard. Yelling at Him at the top of my lungs, shaking my fist at Him, cursing Him, and literally spitting toward heaven, I took all of my desperate frustration out on the one who loves me so much. Knowing full well that God is in control all the time meant that God was the reason for my suffering! How dare he!

It began to rain. The one-sided argument continued well into the evening hours. Soaking wet, exhausted, and utterly overcome with despair, I found myself facedown in the mud crying and asking, "Why?" I had reached rock bottom and had nowhere farther to descend into my anger and blame. I kept waiting for the "burning bush" or the audible voice from above, saying, "My son…" Nothing came. Instead, what did come was an inner voice, a still, small voice that said, and I quote,

> "Are you finished? Do you feel better after throwing your little hissy fit?"

I raised my nose out of the puddle of rainwater that had formed under my body. I looked around the yard, and I was surely alone in my display.

"If you are not finished, I'll wait!"

The inner voice said. I came to my knees and sat in the mud. Sitting in two inches of water, filthy and soaked, I heard the following words as plainly as the words written on this page.

> "If you will trust me, I will get you through this. I am the creator of the universe!
>
> I created you and everything about you.
>
> If you will trust in *me* rather than in *your* understanding, you will see that I have a purpose for you."

All of the arguments I had up to that point seemed to escape me after that. What could I say? I said this, "Okay." There were no formal prayers. No "Blessed Be Thy Name" King James prayers. Just me, sitting in the rain, broken to the core, crying in the arms of the creator of the entire universe. Me and the one who made me.

While sitting in the rain, after having thrown a *world-class* pity party for myself, I was suddenly overcome with a sense of peace, the likes of which I had never felt before. My heart rate slowed, my breathing deepened, and I became calm. I began to finally have thoughts of Christ instead of my own imperfect, flawed, and selfish thoughts. The thought of the sacrifice that Jesus made for me and how much more that He went through, than the "what ifs" I was facing, dwarfed all other thoughts in my mind. The words "No matter what happens, I am in control, and I have you in the palm of my hand" filled every part of me.

Just days later, surgery was scheduled at the House Ear Institute in Los Angeles. House is the institution that literally wrote the book on the procedures used for my type of tumor.

An acoustic neuroma, although noncancerous, is a nasty little thing. Simply stated, it is a disturbance in the myelin, the protective sheath that covers our nerves, on the auditory nerve, which connects our inner ear to our brain. The only *known* cause is a disease called neurofibromatosis. Neurofibromatosis manifests itself in two ways, NF1 and NF2. In a nutshell, neurofibromatosis type 1 is a mutation that causes benign tumors under the skin and along various nerves throughout the body. NF1 was the disease that John Merrick, or "the Elephant Man," was theorized to have had, although that has never been confirmed. NF2 restricts itself to the brain. When a person is diagnosed with NF2 and an acoustic neuroma is present, there is usually a bilateral tumor on the auditory nerve (or one on both sides of the head). In cases such as mine, where there is only a single tumor present, the exact cause is still unknown. I was tested for NF1 and NF2, and the results were negative. A single acoustic neuroma is considered to be a random formation resulting from trauma to the auditory nerve at some point in life. Research is still being conducted; however, they were very interested to learn that my career field had involved exposure to loud noises such as concerts, helicopters, and construction equipment.

In the months leading up to surgery, I was slowly bombarded with images and narratives while I slept. The image of a young man who was fresh from home and who was about to land on the beaches of World War II plagued my mind like an infestation. I could not get the image and developing story out of my mind. I thought that these must just be vivid dreams or random recollections from scenes of a movie. They began to occur every night. Then, they would replay in my head during the day, causing me to become distracted and to daydream.

A cold, wet morning, before the sunrise.

The boats were headed toward the shoreline of the beach in someone else's country.

As I looked to my left, all I could see were dozens of boats just like the one I was on.

As I looked to the right, more boats!

All of the boats were filled with twenty-year-old kids, just like me!

I couldn't hear a thing, not because there was anything going on around me, I couldn't hear anything because everything was drowned out by the sound of my own heart beating.

The boats ran onto the shore.

I swallowed hard!

The gate swung down!

Then…it all began!

This was the beginning of the story that I could not get out of my head. So I decided to get up one night and write the images down. Page after page began to flow from my fingers as I just opened up and let it come out. Five pages! Then ten, fifteen, twenty pages of a story that was coming out of me like an unharnessed fountain. *The Sergeant* was born. After weeks of writing, what would turn into a script, the story was complete. A fictional story of a boy named Pvt. Chambers and his experience with fear, death, chaos, and Christ on the beaches of WWII.

What originally started out as a dream evolved into an obsession. Day after day, my fingers typed. Creativity flowed. What once was a written account of this fictional story soon became a recorded soundtrack designed to become an exercise in visualization. A thirty-minute emotional journey into the unknown with an unforeseen ending. I was inspired. I had never been so inspired in all my life.

> in-spire: The urge or ability to do or feel something, especially to do something creative; To be in the spirit of God (*Webster's Dictionary* 2013)

The Latin root for the word *inspiration* is *spirare*, which means "to breathe." At a time in my life when, according to society, I should have been filled with fear, I was filled with the breath of God. I had never been more creative than during the months leading up to surgery. I wrote and wrote, and stories and narratives such as *The Sergeant*, *Garden Breath*, *Broken*, *The Decision*, and *The Figure at the Wall* were all born at that time. Some were recorded into audio workshops while others remain on paper. The purpose of these stories and their use still remain a mystery. However, I do know this: God has a plan for them! Of this I am sure.

Throughout the process and creative flow I was experiencing through God's inspiration, my faith in Him grew exponentially! My acceptance of His plan for me became my motivation to move forward. I had no idea what His plan was; however, I knew that whatever happened, it would be used to bring glory to Him. There was a better-than-average chance that I could die on the table. If that did not occur, there was an even better possibility that I could have a major stroke and be seriously affected for the rest of my life. I came to accept that if any of these possibilities were to become realities, that God had a reason for it and that somehow good would result because of it.

In early April 2007, I underwent surgery to remove the tumor. It was scheduled to be seven hours long. The surgery went well over that time frame as the doctors were carefully doing their best to separate the tumor from the auditory nerve as well as dozens of smaller nerves that control sensation and function to the right side of my face. Things went far better than anyone had expected—far better than we were told to expect. God was in the room that day. When I awoke from surgery, I realized that God had honored His promise to carry me in the palm of His hand while I was in surgery. To the astonishment of the surgeons, I had no ill effect resulting from the removal of the brain tumor. Aside from the loss of hearing in my right ear, which they knew would happen as a result of the approach they had to take to get the tumor out, and my right eye not tearing when it should, I was going to be okay! Thank you, Lord, for that, by the way! I am a living, breathing, walking miracle of God!

Home a month later, after a spinal fluid leak and recovering to the point where I could travel, I began the long process of rehabilitation: learning how to keep my balance with only half of my equilibrium; building the strength to walk more than a few feet; driving without getting carsick;

and slowly regaining my sense of taste, which took months. I was going to be okay.

What inspires you? What really causes you to stop and take a moment to think? Is it the sunset? Maybe it's sitting on the front porch and watching the dark sky turn pink, then brilliant orange then yellow, as the broken night yields morning light? Maybe it's the sound of the wind singing a song as it blows through the leaves on the trees? What about the majesty of a beautiful mountain range? Or the calming lull of the ocean crashing against the shore? Perhaps it is the soft cooing of your brand-new baby granddaughter? Or perhaps it's love looking back at you through the big brown eyes of the woman you love so much? Maybe it's the achievements of your twenty-two-year-old son, who's only desire is to serve others as a firefighter and as a first responder. Or maybe it's taking delight in the innocence of your seven-year-old daughter's unique view of life? Could it be in watching your twenty-five-year-old daughter become a wonderful mother, and witnessing the drive she has to begin her life, that inspires you? Maybe it's in watching your nineteen-year-old son use his resourcefulness to earn a living and to soar like an eagle? Are you inspired by a brother who has worked all his life to become one of the most respected members in his field, and an amazing dad and husband? Maybe you are inspired by a mother who served as an inspiration to the man who loved her for fifty years. Perhaps it's a dying father who takes his youngest son's hand and says, "Everything is going to be okay" that inspires you? A father who provided for his family by working hard and setting an example for his two young sons to follow? Perhaps it's God who loves you so much that He went through hell on earth and suffered unimaginably because He did not want you to suffer?

I know what inspires me. What inspires you?

Principle 4 of the ARVIS Effect: Inspiration
How to Actually Live, Not Merely Exist

> If all we get out of Christ is a little inspiration
> for a few short years, we're a pretty sorry lot. (1
> Corinthians 15:19, MSG)

I love this translation because it cuts right to the point. The true source of inspiration comes from God. If it is our families, creation, or the sun, or stars, or relationships, it all comes from God. Being inspired is far more than going to church camp and getting caught up in the moment and being on fire for God…for a few weeks. Living life inspired means to seek the little moments right alongside the monumental occasions. There is a movie that I love called *Just Married* (Twentieth Century Fox 2003). In that movie, there is a scene where a father is counseling his son who is distraught because he thinks his marriage is over because he and his (newlywed) wife had a fight. The father said,

> "Son, life is not about the images you see in a photo album. What really matters are the little moments that live between each happy snapshot."

I love that quote! It clearly illustrates the importance of being inspired. It's easy to be inspired when you're sitting on top of the mountain peak looking down at the world below. What about when you're facedown in the rain cursing your very existence and spitting in the face of the one who made you?

Living your life inspired means to appreciate every moment whether good or bad. Giving thanks for the good times *and* the bad. As mentioned at the beginning of this book, God wants to hear us be inspired! He wants to hear us sing in the good times and the bad times. When you are faced with your uphill battle and the "ca-ca is hitting the oscillating air circulation device" and you see no way out, get His "breath!" Talk to God. Tell Him your concerns. Cry, yell, scream, and shout it out! He won't judge you for it. He will *love* you for it because you are talking to Him. You are sharing your soft and vulnerable underbelly with the one who created it. Put your faith in Him and He will inspire you to come closer to Him.

6

S Is for Service!

Harrisburg, Pennsylvania. The trees are a brilliant mix of orange, yellow, and red. The smell of hardwood permeates the air as fireplaces burn nearby. Horses buck and snort as they play in the crisp fall air. Football games abound with the sounds of cheering fans and the fragrance of apple cider and cinnamon fill the air. An average elementary school is in session, and students run from here to there trying to follow the rules. A gathering of five hundred kids from prekindergarten to fifth grade just exited the gymnasium. Equipment and props are being torn down and put away when the rear entrance to the gym opens. In walks a teacher. She is holding the hand of a little brown-haired, brown-eyed girl who could not have been over six years old. She's crying. The teacher is crying. They are walking toward the stage. The side door of the gym opens, and the principal walks in. She has been crying! All three converge at the stage, and the principle says, "Mr. G., this is Maura, and she has something she would like to ask you." Big tears have gathered on her cheeks, and she is still trying to catch her breath through the suppression of her tears. I bend down on one knee and wipe the tears from her cheeks. I am fighting the urge to cry myself. She looks at me, takes a deep breath, then asks me the question that would change my life.

The lines on the road are passing by and are beginning to look more solid than parted. The radio is playing a soft rock tune that was all too familiar to those of us who grew up in the 70s. "I've been through the desert on a horse with no name" (D. Bunnell, America: Warner Brothers Records, 1972) was the soundtrack to the conversation between my father and I. We were on the road to Chicago for a show I had to perform on Monday. It was Saturday afternoon, and he and I were headed north on I-75, and it was a beautiful day. We had just left home a few hours prior, and we were excited about the forty-five-day journey that we were embarking on.

You see, after my surgery, and a year of seeking God, I made good on my bargain with Him. *God, if you let me live through this and somehow I am still functional, in some way, I promise I will do whatever you ask and I will go wherever you send me!* (Warning: Be careful what you wish for! God remembers what you say!)

One year after my recovery, I began having the desire to give back because I had been given so much. God gave me my life, my health, and a near total recovery from what was supposed to be a life-altering brain tumor. It was life-altering all right, but not in the way we all thought. I began to pay attention to the tourist industry that I had been a part of for many years. The Great Smoky Mountains of East Tennessee is not only known for its beautiful mountains, parks, rivers, fishing, and recreation, it's also known for its theaters and shows. Having been in the lighting and sound industry all my life, I was well aware of the spirit and theme that the shows in town had. Even though they were all family- or kid-"friendly," none were written specifically for kids. I would watch as they would sit with their heads in their hands because they did not understand the songs or the drama that was unfolding on the stage before them. They were bored!

One afternoon, God put it in my heart to do something about it. I could not shake the feeling that I was supposed to make a difference somehow. I consulted my best friend, David Major, who is a megatalented producer, entertainer, and creative genius. Together we began brainstorming, writing, and ultimately created Scream N' Shout Interactive Kids Show.

It was a one-of-a-kind production in that we took my years of technical know-how, equipment, and skill and coupled it with David's creativity and brilliant adaptation of dance, choreography, and personal interaction—all these resulted in a show that was designed specifically for young children. With high hopes, and dreams of making a difference, we debuted the show at a major attraction in Pigeon Forge, Tennessee. It was a huge success, and we thought, "Here we go! We are going to be able to make a difference now!" Well…not so much as it would turn out.

Even though the show was a major hit with test audiences, the venue had difficulty trying to incorporate it into their existing theater schedule. Scream N' Shout never got off the ground! Or so it would seem. Because of obligations back home, David had to return to California, and back to our lives we went. I was devastated. I could not believe that all of our hard work was gone! David was working back in Cali, and I was doing the same old things in Tennessee. I decided that I was not going to let SNS die without a fight. I began to approach everyone I knew and pitched the idea of bringing the show to their facility. Rejection after rejection came, and it was very difficult not to get discouraged. *God! What are you doing wrong?* I would shout out with a smile on my face. Finally, one day, it happened! The phone rang! "We want to give your show a test run," the voice on the phone said. "I have a strip shopping center, and I am going to give you the space and pay the bills for one year so your show will have a fighting chance." What! I could not believe it! Tell me that God doesn't answer prayers! The Scream N' Shout Theater was born! We did it! The theater was a success, and I thought that I was fulfilling my promise to God. Little did I know that this was only a stepping stone to something much bigger.

One day, I was doing some preproduction work in the theater when the door opened and a man walked in and introduced himself as an entertainer in the next town of Gatlinburg. I was familiar with his show and was curious to learn more about it. He and I struck up a conversation, and to make a long story short, we became friends. After seeing each other's show(s), several times, I began consulting with him and he with me. He told me, "Man, you should really consider taking this show into the schools!" He planted the seed, and for that, I will always be grateful to him!

Enter Scream N' Shout "Kidz with Character," a character-building assembly that focuses on the six pillars of character! It was an adapted version of the original show and would eventually grow to become one of the most requested elementary school assemblies in the country. SNS "KWC" would take me to all lower forty-eight states many times, and I found myself traveling ten months of the year. I have had the privilege of speaking to tens of thousands of students at hundreds of schools about the importance of living their life with character! "Doing the right thing even when no one is looking, and you are not going to get credit for it" was the core theme of the forty-five-minute assembly.

It was on many of these trips that I had the privilege of taking my father along with me. On this particular trip, I was going to be gone for forty-five days or more and was going to be traveling to many states that my father had never seen. I approached him and asked if he would like to accompany me on this trip. I cautioned him that we would be gone a while but we would travel to parts of the country he has always wanted to see. I knew he wanted to go, but he told me he would talk it over with my mother and let me know. Of course, my mother, being the awesome wife and mother she is, already had his bags packed and sent him on this once-in-a-lifetime journey with his number 2 son.

We had the best time on that trip. My father got to watch me serve thousands of kids by teaching them the value and importance of being responsible, respectful, reliable, trustworthy, to be good citizens, and to care about themselves as well as others. I knew he was proud. The students loved my dad! Although he would sit quietly in the back of the room or to the side of the stage, he would smile and clap along with the students. He didn't realize it, but he was showing each and every one of those kids what it means to serve! Let me explain.

All throughout my childhood and teenage years, my dad served others. Not in the traditional sense of serving food in a soup kitchen, although he did do that from time to time. The service I am referring to is helping others. My dad was the type of man who would call an employee into his office and close the door. Of course, the employee might have thought that he had done something wrong. But that was not the case. One time, my father called an employee into his office and simply handed him some money and said, "I want you to take this because I know that you need it." You see, this employee was trying to build a home for his family, and he had no money to buy a refrigerator, stove, or washer and dryer. My father knew this, and he could not stand by and let this family go without when God had blessed his family so much.

With tears in his eyes, and a heart as big as Texas, my father served that man. He served his family, and to this day, that employee tears up when he talks about the impact Smitty had on his life. That is what service is all about, my friends. Ricky, my dad loved you, brother!

One day, while on this forty-five-day trek across the country, my father and I found ourselves in Casper, Wyoming. We had stopped for lunch at a small roadside truck stop. We went inside, and Flo (not kidding, that was her real name!) took our order. As we sat in the broken-down booth, my dad looked out the window at the great plains of wheat grass that swayed in the wind like a vast ocean and said, "This reminds me of a truck stop I was at a long time ago." I said, "Really? What were you doing? Where was it?" He said, "It was in west Texas, and it was when you were little. I was on my way home from a job, and I stopped in to get a bite to eat, and that place looked a lot like this one, only the fields were desert, not grass!" He then went on to tell me a story about something that happened to him at that truck stop.

> "I was sitting at my booth eating my lunch when I noticed a man across the room, and he was sitting alone. I could not tell much about him, but something kept my eyes focused in his direction. I continued with my meal and soon forgot about the man. After I was finished eating, I got up and went to go use the restroom."

At this point, my father's speech changed. His voice got softer, and he began to look down at his hands, which were nervously rubbing one another. His eyes began to well with tears, and his voice broke as he continued his story.

> "When I entered the restroom, I noticed that someone was already occupying the stall, so I patiently waited. In just a few moments, I heard what sounded

like rustling noises coming from the stall, and eventually the man who had been sitting across the room came out of the stall. It was obvious at that point that this man was physically challenged to quite a severe degree. He was having difficulty negotiating the narrow walkway and maintaining his stability. We spoke, and he was very nice and refused my offer to assist, however I may have been able.

We offered cordial smiles as we each went back to our booths. I watched as the waitress brought him his bill. He dug in his pockets for whatever change he could find, and it appeared to me that he either did not have enough to pay the bill or had just enough to pay the bill, as there was a short conversation as she took the payment to the cash register. He got up from his seat and went outside to get in his car, I assumed. I paid my bill and went on out to my truck. As I went to get into my truck, I happened to glance in the direction he left in and noticed that he was walking (as best he could) down this hot, dusty highway."

At this point, my father could not hold back his emotions. His voice broke, and he apologized for his emotional display. Of course I was touched by the compassion I could hear in his voice as he recounted this apparently life-changing moment. With red, tear-filled eyes, shaky voice, and guarded self-consciousness, Dad continued his story.

> "At this point, I knew that this man had no car and was attempting to walk to wherever it was he was trying to go. I knew the next town was thirty-eight miles away!
>
> I ran over to him and said, 'Excuse me, sir. Is there someplace I can take you?'
>
> The man said, 'Naw...I'm okay.' I said, 'Well, I don't know you, and you don't know me, but I feel that I am supposed to give you this,' and I handed the man a $100 bill. The man broke down and cried right there on the side of the road. It was obvious that this man was down on his luck, and he simply needed someone to care. I cared!"

The compassion I saw in my father during that story just about brought me to my knees. You see, I was aware of my dad's capacity and desire to serve others because I had been witness to it all my life. However, this story was special to my dad. He told me that he had not told many people about the man because people can be so cruel. He told me that one person said, "Oh, Smitty! You're a sucker! You know that guy was just playing you and is just going to go drink that hundred dollars!" The cool thing about my father was that he knew that what the man did with that money was not my father's concern. The disposition of that money was between the man and God. Not the man and my dad. God commands us to give.

Deuteronomy 15:10 (NIV) says, "Give generously to him and do so without a grudging heart; then because of this the Lord your God will bless you in all your work and in everything you put your hand to."

Giving freely, that is, with no expectation of anything in return, is one of the purest examples of serving someone. All too often we give with strings. Oh, we may not think so, but let me ask you a question: Have you ever done something for someone and gotten offended because they didn't say, "Thank you"? True service to someone is giving, and still loving them, even when they spit in your face instead of saying thank-you! Can you do that? I know I can't! Not by my own strength for sure!

As I looked into her big brown eyes, lips quivering, and her breathing short and shallow, I asked her, "Maura, what would you like to ask me?" I could hear the sniffs of both her teacher and the principal as they waited for the question. It took her a minute, but she finally pulled herself together enough to say these words:

"Mr. G.? Do you *really* think that even I could be something someday?"

My heart broke! I was instantly overcome by a huge lump in my throat, and it took everything I had to keep my voice steady and solid. I put my hands on her shoulders and said, "Maura, I absolutely *know* that you can be whatever you want to be when you grow up!" By this time, the teacher and the principal were barely holding their composure because they knew what was coming next.

"Mr. G.? During the assembly, you looked at me and you said you didn't see a kid, that you saw a doctor. Is that true?"

During the assembly, there is a portion toward the end where I have the kids look around the room and tell me what they see. Their response is always, "KIDS!" I tell them that "when Mr. G. looks around the room, I do not see kids at all. I see doctors, lawyers, teachers, astronauts, race car drivers, athletes, scientists," etc. I looked at her and said,

"Maura, you could absolutely be the best doctor that the world has ever seen if you work hard and you try your very best!"

At this point, I saw the teacher and principal put one hand each on Maura's shoulders as they braced themselves for her third and final question. Her eyes filled up with tears, and she started to cry. She spoke these words through pain and sadness.

> "Mr. G.? Do you think that I could grow up and become a doctor in time to save my mommy?"

Oh God! Oh God! Oh God! Help me say the right thing to this little girl! I shouted to God in the quiet of my thoughts. I could not say the wrong thing to her! If I said one thing, it could dash her hopes of keeping her obviously terminal mother. If I said another, I could give her false hope that she might be able to intervene somehow. *What do I say, God? She's waiting for an answer!* Nothing came. I sat there with my hands on her shoulders and wiping away her tears for what seemed like an hour. In reality, it was about thirty seconds when these words came from the still, small voice that I have come to rely so heavily upon,

> "Maura honey, your mommy doesn't need you to be a doctor. You see, your mommy already has the best doctors in the world taking care of her! What your mommy needs from you is for you to be the best Maura you can be! She needs you to love her, lay

with her, talk to her, and tell her all about your day at school. She needs you to laugh and tell her what funny things you have done. Maura, she needs you to be her little girl! I bet you're very good at being her little girl, aren't you?"

Her little face lit up! She smiled as big as the sky and shook her head and said, "Uh-huh! She loves to see what I color, and she laughs when I do this!" (She shakes her head and makes a funny noise.)

"See! You are already doing what you are supposed to be doing!"

"Let the doctors do what doctors are supposed to do, and you do what Maura is supposed to do!" I said.

With that statement, she hugged my neck with the force of a ten-ton press and ran back to class shouting, "I'm gonna color my mom a new picture!" She left the gym, and the door closed behind her, and I broke down and cried like a baby. All three of us were sobbing at the heartbreak that Maura was trying to deal with in her young mind.

It was then that the teacher told me that Maura's mother had stage 4 breast cancer and was predicted to not survive the month. She followed by telling me that when her mother entered the hospital that her father decided that then would be a good time to start molesting Maura. The authorities stepped in and removed her from her home and placed her in foster care. The first foster family proceeded to tell her that she was worthless and that it was *her* fault that her mommy was sick! They removed her from that home, and the new foster family was giving her the love and support that she needs; however, she's only been in that new foster home for a week.

The statement that followed provided the confirmation that God is totally in control and that I was where I was supposed to be. The principal said to me,

> "You see, Mr. G., Maura has been through more than a lifetime's worth of pain at her young age. We, at the school, are the only means of consistent support and love that she gets now that her mother is fading. We're it! Today, you came to this school, and you gave that girl hope when unscrupulous people have robbed all hope from her! You did not give her false hope that she could change her mother's health! You gave her hope that she can be more than what she's been told she is. You gave Maura permission to be a little girl again! We tell her how special and wonderful she is every day. However, she sees us every day, so it does not have much of an impact. Here you come, and to her, you are a rock star! You looked her in the eyes, and you told her, 'You can

be somebody,' when everyone she knows has told her she is nothing! You have changed that girl's life! Thank you! And please do not ever stop doing what you are doing!"

Of course, at that point, I was speechless and emotionally drained. *What just happened here?* I thought to myself. I'm just a regular guy! I'm not a minister or a preacher! I don't have the credentials that some professor of psychology may have! I'm just me! Your basic "boogerhead!" But you know what? God was in that gym that day. He used me, an ordinary nobody, to do an extraordinary thing for that little girl. God changed that little girl's life that day, not Guy Michaels. He may have spoken through me, but make no mistake, I was *freaking out*, so God had to do all the talking!

> ser-vice: An act of assistance or benefit; a favor. An offering of goodwill for the benefit of others (*Webster's Dictionary* 2013)

The point of this story is to illustrate the importance of service to others. The world preaches to serve yourself because no one else will. "I have to get mine while I can!" is the attitude of far too many people in this world. By figuring out that true happiness lies in giving happiness away, we open ourselves up to the warehouse of blessings that God has for us.

I am reminded of a story that I was told a long time ago.

> There is a man who has followed Jesus as best he could all of his life. One day, Jesus decides to call him home. When the man arrives at the pearly gates of heaven, he is greeted by Jesus himself! With arms stretched wide, he embraces the man and welcomes him home! As they enter the gates of heaven, the man sees that heaven is more beautiful than he had ever imagined! The words could not find his lips when he would try to say how wonderful a place heaven really was. As Jesus took him on a personal tour, they ended up in the countryside. Beautiful mountains and trees and lakes and rivers! Animals everywhere! It was beautiful. As they walked, the man was asking Jesus all the questions that he had been wanting to ask since he was a little boy. As they were talking, they came upon an area where there were large warehouses that blanketed the landscape for as far as the eye could see. From horizon to horizon were these huge buildings.
>
> The man asked, "What are these buildings, Lord?"
> Jesus said, "Come inside, I'll show you."

When the man looked up at the entrance to this particular building, he noticed a big sign that had *his* name on it! They entered. As they walked inside this building, the man could see neither the side walls nor the end of the building. It was so large, the edges could not be seen. As they walked, the man observed thousands of feet of shelving that stored box after box after box. Some were small and some were huge! Finally the curiosity got the better of the man, and he stopped and asked, "Jesus, what are all these boxes doing in this building with my name on it? There are so many, there is no possible way they could be counted? What is this place? And why is my name on the outside of this building?

Jesus paused for a moment, then looked sadly at the floor. With sadness in his voice, he said, "This is the warehouse where I store all the blessings that I have for you."

The man said, "Yes, Lord...but what are all these boxes that stretch on for as far as I can see?"

Jesus said, "Those are all the blessings that you never asked for."

Have you asked for the blessings that God has stored up for you? If you haven't, you should. By being a blessing to someone else and by serving others, we are blessed in return. Giving someone money when they need it is a blessing to them and to you. Do not be concerned with what they are going to do with the money. That is between them and God. Let God worry about what happens next. Say a kind word to someone just because you can. Bless them with kindness and you, in turn, will be blessed.

Principle 5 of the ARVIS Effect: Service If You Want More Happy? Give It Away!

God is not unjust; he will not forget your work and the love you have shown him as you have helped his people and continue to help them. (Hebrews 6:10, niv)

There is a song by the Gaither Vocal Band with the words "If you want more happy…give it away" (G. Gaither and B. Gaither, Gaither Vocal Band, "Give It Away," 2006). That says just that! If we want happiness in our lives, the quickest way to achieve it is to give happiness to someone else. If we can just learn that the true nature of happiness is in the service of someone other than ourselves, we would soon find that our lives are overcome with joy and gratitude. Of course, there are times when we are just not happy and the last thing on our minds is to try to make someone else happy! That is an even better time to try to serve someone else because when we are in the service of others, we soon forget about whatever we are not currently happy about.

Let's talk about the ultimate act of service. Before Jesus went to the cross, Jesus told all of his disciples to remove their sandals because Jesus was going to wash their feet. Think about that for a moment. Personally, I am not a fan of feet. I think there is a reason that God put them on the bottom of the body and covered them with shoes! However, by today's standards, our feet are made of gold compared to the feet of people two thousand years ago. Their feet had to be nasty! Dirty, smelly, and gross, and Jesus "The lord of lords and the king of kings is going to wash *my* feet? Oh no, you're not!" they proclaimed. Jesus then spoke to them about the importance of being in service to one another. If Jesus Christ can stoop to the floor and wash someone's nasty feet, can we not speak a kind word to someone even when we don't feel like it? Can we not give someone a dollar and bless them and not be concerned with their intended use of our "hard-earned money"? Being a servant to others and humbling ourselves for a moment will open the door to unimaginable joy. We may not see it in the short term, but the promise is there. Give happiness to someone else and be a blessing to them. Put yourself aside and think about someone else, and it will come back to you tenfold.

7

THE WONDERFUL
WORLD OF WALTER

La Jolla, California, in February 2011. It is one of the prettiest afternoons I can remember in a long time. The California sun is shining brightly, and the cool sea breeze is whipping through the trees and cooling the joggers passing by. A small strip-shopping center is my destination as I spot a place for lunch. Hungry, I feel the pangs for pizza and pull into the parking lot. I sit in my truck for fifteen minutes contemplating this decision: Do I go in? Do I move on?

Driving through the mountains of Colorado, my family was heading out on our very first ski trip in Colorado. Excited, my brother and I rode in the backseat anticipating what this experience would be like. The hum of the tires against the pavement and the *thump thump thump* of the right rear tire as it hit the outermost edge of the lane induced us all into the "highway hypnosis" that we've all experienced from time to time. Breckenridge is the destination, and we are ready to go!

As daylight gives way to darkness, the stars shine bright as the sun because there is absolutely no light pollution contaminating the night sky. The snow is falling so heavily that our car is now moving at an absolute crawl. "Finally!" my father said with relief in his voice. It had been a long trip from Dallas, Texas, to our resort getaway! Tensions were high as my father had been concentrating on keeping us safe in the treacherous snow and ice. We were all glad to be there!

The car pulls into the parking lot of the hotel, and we all sat in the car for a second surveying the "dream destination" of the hotel as conveyed by its advertisements. Without going into much detail, as I was just a little kid at the time, suffice it to say that at this point in our nation's history, there was no such thing as TripAdvisor, Yelp, or even the Internet for that matter. Had there been? We would have ended up somewhere else! The outside of the "hotel" would have been more accurately described as a place with the motto "Stay at Ed's! Or not! We could really care less!"

From the backseat, I could see my father look at my mother, and even though I could not hear their words, I could totally tell what they were saying! The decision was made to give it a try since we were so tired and all we wanted to do was go to bed! My father opened his car door and slowly disappeared into the snowfall as he made his way toward the front door. After a few minutes of idle chatter between my brother and I, my father returned with key in hand! The car was quickly relocated to the spot designated for the room we had been assigned, and in we went. The interior of the room was quite underwhelming aside from the interesting white liquid dripping from the ceiling. We were so tired, all we were concerned with (at the moment) was going to bed; and seeing as the "mystery drip" was nowhere near our beds, we didn't worry about it, at least for this night.

As time progressed, the issues became worse as we noticed a cold chill wafting through the room from time to time. "Where is that coming from?" Dad asked himself while mumbling under his breath. My father was doing his very best to keep his cool so his family could have a great time from the very first moment! This task was becoming increasingly difficult as my dad noticed where the draft was coming from. Upon looking in the direction of the door, we noticed that we could see the light from the parking lot coming from the three-inch gap under the door to the room.

I could tell that my father had had enough at that point. He picked up the phone and called the front desk and was apparently greeted by an individual who was less than sympathetic to our cause.

"We are full. Sorry," he said to my father, whose face was growing ever more intense by the second.

"Well if you are full, we want our money returned to us!" my father said.

"No refunds!" the voice on the other end of the phone said, while being devoid of all emotion.

My father put the phone back on the receiver, and with one hand on the phone, the other hand on his hip, and his head looking down toward the floor, he took a deep breath and just stared into space for a moment. "I'll be right back!" he said as he walked out the door that had the custom "air-conditioning" feature built right in!

After what seemed to be an hour passed, my father returned. In truth, it was more like ten minutes, but my preteen imagination was getting the best of me as I wondered what was going on in the office at that time. When he returned, he had cash in hand and said, "Let's go! We are going somewhere else!" We packed back up and found a great place just down the road and ended up having the time of our lives! It was a great ending to an otherwise rocky beginning.

I do not really know what happened in the office of that motel that night. I never really thought any more of it until many years later when my father and I were on one of my cross-country treks with Scream N' Shout. In one of our many conversations, we got on the subject of some of the ski trips we all went on as a family.

"Since we are on the subject, Dad...do you remember that first trip to Colorado and the awful room?"

"Sure!" he said.

"When you went to have a chat with the clerk at the front desk, what happened that night? All we knew was that you were told *no*! Then you went to see him, then you returned with all your money in hand? What did you say to him?"

At that point, my father took a long breath and began to tell me of his emotions that night. He told me how excited he had been to take his family on a new experience. That he was proud and was ready to have a good time with his wife and kids. When seeing what the place actually looked like versus what it looked like in the pictures, he began to become angry. He did not want his family's vacation ruined by someone else's misrepresentation of the facts. He went on to tell me that when we entered the room, and seeing the dripping mystery substance and then the gap under the door, that he just lost his cool. Dad went on to tell me that when he spoke to the young clerk and upon hearing the attitude coming from the phone, that he totally lost his cool and was going to "correct" the situation himself.

My dad had never been a violent man, and I knew that he would have never physically harmed anyone in any way.

So I was curious how he "corrected" the situation. "What did you say to him?" I asked. Suffice it to say that my father let me know that he was very direct with his words to the clerk. Whatever he said to him must have been effective because the clerk returned his money and the situation was over. Or was it?

Over twenty years after that ski trip, my father and I are having this conversation. As he is telling me his perspective of the situation, I could see his demeanor change. He began to look toward the floorboard of the truck, and I could tell that he was bothered by something.

"What is it, Dad?" I asked.

"That has always bothered me."

"What has always bothered you?" I asked.

"The way I let the circumstances govern how I felt on the inside. I let things beyond my control dictate the things I could control."

"What do you mean?" I asked.

"I could not control that the place was a dump. I could not control that the clerk had an attitude and most likely just wanted to go home to his family. However, I could have controlled the way I reacted to it. I could have remembered that we—my family and the clerk—were not the only ones involved in that situation. I forgot that He"—pointing his finger toward heaven—"was watching. He couldn't have been very happy with me that day."

I said, "Dad, what did God see you do that day?"

He said, "He saw me lose my cool as I threatened to go over that counter and 'convince' him to give me my money back. I scared that poor kid to death. I would have never gotten physical with that clerk, but I sure wanted to!"

I could tell that this incident has weighed on my father's mind for years. He knew that God was just shaking His head with His arms crossed across His chest as Dad lost his cool. God spoke to my father that night. The still, small voice that lived inside my father spoke up on that night, and my father heard it. I learned a lot about my dad during that conversation. Not that my dad can lose his cool, like we all do, but that my dad knew when God was talking to him and that he also knew when he was ignoring God's voice.

It's summertime in Southern California, and I am packing up my equipment and loading the truck after having met and ministered to one thousand amazing kids at a local elementary school. I use the word *ministered* because even though I never mention God or being a Christian in my assemblies for the public school systems across the country (for obvious reasons), I always knew that if someone was in tune with God, that they could tell where my heart truly lies.

As I was putting my equipment in the truck, I was approached by a teacher who said, "Mr. G.? You are a Christian, aren't you?"

I looked at her for a moment and wondered if I had misspoken during the assembly or had somehow let it slip that I was a Christian. "Yes, ma'am, I sure am, why do you ask?" I replied.

"I could just tell," she said. "There was something about the way you spoke to the kids. The way you connected with them and the hope and self-esteem you instilled in them just reminded me of the way I would imagine Jesus being with them. Laughing with them, telling them how much God loves them. How unique and special each and every one of them are to Him. I saw a spark in you, Mr. G., don't let that go," she said.

I am reminded of a song by Carman called "Some-O-Dat" (Carman, "Some-O-Dat," Sony Records, 1991) that's words say…

> Well I got this friend named T. J. Clyde who sees this strength of God inside
>
> So he says to me, "Hey, I want some-o-dat." I say, "Clyde, it's easy as one, two, three, you just say this simple prayer with me." He said, "Not me, bubba, but I still want Some-O-Dat."

Well I was sharing with this salesman, Lyle, so he says with a million-dollar smile,

"Why, that's interesting you know. Hey, I'd like some-o-dat." I said, "Lyle, you're gonna have to humble your pride and ask the Lord to come inside." He said, "No-

ho-ho-ho, but I still want some-o-dat."

Well you can't find it in astrology, that horoscope that you read is just a waste

You can't find it looking at the stars Jupiter, the moon, and Mars.

'Cause you'll soon find that all you got was space.

Well my best friend Ray has got this niece that sees within my eyes this peace.

And yesterday she said, "I want some-o-dat."

I said, "Hey, sugar, now, it's a breeze. Just talk with Jesus on your knees."

She said, "I'm not the type, but I still want some-o-dat."

Brother, you can't find it in a bottle or even when you pop a pill or two

You can't find it smoking dope or weed 'cause one fine day you're gonna see

That the dope that's being smoked, my friend, is you!

> Well if you're depressed then get used to it 'cause
> without Jesus, you have blew it
>   He's the only one who can give you some-o-dat!
>   Why not try the Lord for goodness' sake you'll
> be happy as a dog with a T-bone
>   Steak, then you can say, "HEY, I got some-o-dat!

The words she spoke to me were more of a compliment than I could have ever hoped for. She confirmed that (at least that day) Christ could be seen through me. Being a Christian means so much more than simply knowing who Jesus Christ was or is, depending on your beliefs. It's more than knowing the stories of the Bible and acknowledging that there "may" be a God. Being a true Christian involves many levels of faith, self-awareness, willingness to submit, willingness to speak (and *hear*) the truth, even when it hurts! True Christianity is when the Holy Spirit takes up residence inside you and begins to slowly transform the old and dried up you into a new and fresh you. Much like reversing the process of a grape becoming a raisin; even though the raisin is sweet, it is not the intended form of that fruit! Jesus can rehydrate the sweet raisin and restore it to an even sweeter grape! The way it was intended! A true Christian does not need to stand on the street corner and proclaim to the world, "Look how Christian I am." Nor do they need to warm a church pew every Sunday when their hearts know that they should be serving someone in need. If Christ truly lives inside you, others can tell. They can see it, sense it, feel it! Well…at least most of the time.

Now, I am in no way saying that a Christian does not need to attend church. I am saying, however, that the four walls of brick and mortar do not define you as a true Christian. True "church" can be held on the side of a road as you assist someone in need while ten thousand people sit in a sports arena doing nothing for the kingdom of God. Christianity should be seen in who you are and not just in how you act.

After packing my truck and leaving for the next school, I was "high" on her words of compliment and soon found myself hungry. Being on the road for so long, your average fast-food place tends to become a very familiar friend! Although the reality is they are really no friend at all.

Driving down the highway, I came across a sign that said "Pizza Hut 5 Miles." *Hmmm, I have not had pizza in a while, I think I will go there!* I thought. As I pulled into the parking lot and prepared to exit my truck, I happened to look toward the entrance of the restaurant. It was located in a strip shopping center and had windows all across the front. The windows were about three feet off the ground and were sitting on a concrete block wall. Sitting in front of the concrete wall and not six inches from the entrance was one of the dirtiest and most disheveled-looking man

I had ever seen. He was sitting on the ground with what appeared to be *all* of his earthly possessions by his side in what looked like a shopping cart that had also seen better days. I was too far away to hear his voice, but I could see that as people would come near, he would raise his hand and say something to them. Of course I had no idea what he was saying, but my imagination ran wild!

Oh, here we go! I'm not even going to be able to eat lunch without being hassled! The management should do something! I just want to eat! Why can't I just eat without being bothered every time I turn around! Come on, man! Are you kidding me! Jesus Christ! was my internal dialogue.

Remember, not an hour prior, I was being praised by a teacher for exhibiting Christ through my demeanor and my actions! As I write this story, I am ashamed of the way I allowed my thoughts to negate everything that teacher observed! God was watching. He was surely disappointed in me in that point. I truly believe He decided to teach me a lesson at that moment. (Read on. You will love what happens next as I totally get put in my place.)

I decided that I was hungry enough to deal with being "harassed" by this homeless guy. I walked toward the entrance, and as I got closer, I could see that this man had not bathed in weeks. His face looked as though he had recently changed the oil in someone's car and used his face as the oil pan! His clothes were "stiff" with sweat and dirt and smelled like something out of a science fiction novel! His shoes had holes so large I could see his bare toes (with those gross "old man" toenails) in clear view. To his left was a shopping cart that had three wheels and was full of what looked to me like random pieces of paper, cans, cardboard, an old blanket, and who knows what else. He had a ragged old watch cap on his head that covered shoulder-length silver hair that looked to have not been washed since the 80s. His beard had "stuff" in it that I could not recognize.

As I approached, I decided to just pretend he was not there and walked right by him as he held his hand up in my direction. I thought to myself, *I'm hungry and tired, and I have a* long *trip ahead of me, and I don't have time for this nonsense! Surely this guy could get a job somewhere! I work hard for my money! Why should I just give it to this guy! I already gave to the last guy! And the guy before that! No! Not this time!* as I walked by with eyes straight ahead and a sense of purpose in my step! He said nothing as I walked past as though he were an insect.

As I sat down, I was greeted by a nice server who took extra-special care to ensure my time there was pleasurable. The food was *hot* and *fresh* and was just what I wanted after performing and "showing the light of Christ to one thousand kids!" Right? Not! What a mockery I was making of myself at that very moment. As I would eat, I could not keep my eyes off the entrance to the restaurant. All I could see was the back of the brick wall that obscured the home-less man from my view. The only thing I could see was the very top of his tattered watch cap and his hand as he would raise it toward people passing by.

The more I looked in that general direction, the more God started to "jerk a knot in my chain," as my father used to say. I began to have the thoughts, *"Get a to-go box and give him your leftovers." "NO!"* I hollered at my internal dia-logue! *"I'm not going to do it!"* I said to myself. Well, do you remember when I said, "When God has a hold of your life and you run from Him, you ultimately run into Him"? That happened to me at that moment. My thoughts shifted from taking this man my leftovers to purchasing a fresh new pizza and a drink to give to him. *All right, God! You win! I'll do it! Dang it!* as I ordered a large thin-crust supreme with a large Mountain Dew to go!

As the food was delivered to my table, I paid my check and prepared to leave the building. Upon approaching the exit, I contemplated how I was going to give this food to this man without having to be "bothered" by him. I walked out the door. I stood beside him looking straight ahead, not acknowledging him for at least a minute. Finally I turned my head toward him and shifted my eyes in his direction. When I focused in on him, he was already looking into my eyes.

He's going to ask me for money! Or he's going to beg! Ugh! I thought to my "uber Christian" self as I waited for him to speak. Again, as I sit and write this chapter, my disgust for myself, at that moment, continues to grow! Oh, what a hypocrite I was. He reached his hand up and actually touched my left hand. He took a deep breath. *Here it comes!* I thought. He opened his mouth and spoke these words.

> "Excuse me, sir, do you think you could spend a lit-
> tle time with me?"

At that very moment, God reached down and *slapped* me upside the face with a two-by-four of shame! I was literally humiliated at how I had been thinking and acting while riding the wave of misguided praise I had received earlier. I was crushed under the weight of my own arrogance. This man wanted *nothing* from me other than for someone to just spend a little time with him. He wanted someone to put themselves aside for a moment and just talk.

I was broken. I was humiliated. I was embarrassed. I was ashamed. *Who's high and mighty now?* I said to myself with contempt for my own existence.

I said with a broken voice, under the conviction of the Holy Spirit, "Yes, sir, I will spend as much time with you as you would like," and I sat down beside him. Still shaking my head as to how much of a horse's backside I had been. He asked with a smile, "Is that for me?" while pointing to the pizza box and soft drink in my hand. "Yes, sir, it is," I said. Eagerly he took the soda and took a long swig from the straw. "Mmm, Mountain Dew! My favorite!" he shouted. He opened the box and smelled the aroma of the peppers, olives, ground beef, and all the fixin's like it was the sweetest smell in the world. He took his hand and pulled out the biggest slice and offered it to *me*! What a jerk I had been! This man who has nothing compared to me was offering me the first portion of what could have been his only meal in days! As it turned out, this man had *more* than I could ever hope to gain! He was rich far beyond what I could possibly imagine! This man had more to offer me than I could have ever offered him.

"My name is Walter," he said.

"Hi, Walter, I'm Guy. It's very nice to meet you."

Walter began eating and telling me about his day and all the people he had come into contact with. With a mouth full of pizza and tomato sauce joining the myriad of other substances now residing in his silver- and dirt-colored beard, he said, "Most folks walk by and don't even act like I am here, much like you did." Guilt and shame flooded my face. "But you know what? They have places to be and lives to live!"

"Walter, what's your story, man? How did you end up like this?" I asked.

While firmly entrenched into his third piece of pizza, he answered, "Well, back in the day, I was a drummer for a well-known country artist." (He told me the name, and I was floored! During our conversation, I actually Googled an old album cover of this artist and saw a much younger version of Walter right there on the cover!) "Let's just say that I was not living my life right. I was married and had two older sons, but I was on the road a lot, and well, you know, I wasn't doing the right thing by my family. I was actually a pretty despicable person to be honest. You see, I claimed to be a Christian. Do you know Jesus?" he asked.

I was ashamed to answer given how I had been acting but said, "Yes, sir, I do."

He continued, "Well, God knew what I was doing, and I guess he just wanted to teach me a lesson."

"In what way?" I asked.

"Well, my family life was all but destroyed by my actions on the road, and one day I decided that I wanted to try to put my family back together. I quit the band and called my sons who agreed to come to the city we had been performing in and pick me up. When they arrived, I put my suitcase in the car and off we went. I was trying to talk to them, but they were quiet because I had been such a poor example all their lives, and I could tell they were doing this out of obligation. We were in North Carolina at the time, and we were headed cross-country toward California. Long about El Paso, Texas, we stopped at one of those roadside rest stops, and we all went in to use the bathroom. When I came out, my two sons and their car were gone. I thought to myself, I wonder what happened? Where could they be? I waited until dark, but they never returned. This was in the mid-1980s, and I have never heard from them since."

I asked, "Well, Walter, did something happen to them? Are they okay?"

He replied, "Yes, they were fine. That was their plan all along. They wanted to abandon me as I had abandoned them. I've tried for years to contact them and the rest of my family, but no one is interested."

I said, "Walter, how long have you been without a home or family?"

He said, "Since that day."

To make a long story short, Walter told me his entire life story. He told me of various opportunities to pull himself out of poverty and how they failed one by one. He told me of the harsh words he heard from family and friends as he tried to get help. He told me of the "payback" he was receiving from those he had done so wrong years prior. Then he told me something that brought me to my spiritual knees!

"You know, Guy, I've been to hell and back, and it's because I lost sight of the prize! I lost focus on what was truly important. I forgot that way back in the 60s, I gave my heart to Jesus, and from that point on, I was a child of the king. You know, Guy, that when you are a child of the king that you can't get away from Him even if you try? I turned my back on God, but God never turned His back on me!"

This coming from a man who has been homeless for over twenty years!

"How has God not turned His back on you, Walter? You have been homeless for over twenty years! You have no home! You have no money! You have no food! You probably don't have a place to sleep tonight! You don't have anything!" I said with passion in my voice.

"He didn't leave me back then, Guy, I left him behind. I lost it all. However, that doesn't mean I have nothing! I've got God, man, and that's all I need," he said as he finished his fourth piece of pizza. "I turned my back on God for sure, but God never forgot me. Even though you are correct in that I do not have any money, I do not have any food, and yes, I do not know where I am going to sleep tonight, you are wrong in one thing: I do have a home! My home is wherever God is. He never lets me down. When I need a dry place to sleep, He provides a bridge at just the right time! When I am thirsty, He provides the rain. When I am tired, He gives me the strength to keep on truckin'. And… you know what, Guy? when I was hungry, he provided *you*! I have all I need, man, because God has all of me."

This man had *nothing* by almost anyone's standards, including my own. Yet Walter had more riches than could be counted or measured. He had the creator of the universe in his heart, and that was good enough for him. I spent almost nine hours with Walter that day, and well into the night, sitting right there in front of a Pizza Hut in La Jolla, California, during the spring of 2011. God went to Pizza Hut that day, and my life was changed.

"Walter, I travel the country doing elementary school assemblies. Chances are that I am headed somewhere near some family or friends. Is there anyplace I can take you?" I asked.

"Naw…there is no one, and besides, I have all I need right here." Pointing to his shopping cart that contained everything he owned.

I told him, "I have food, water, blankets, pillows, a portable radio, and lots of batteries that I would like to give you, if you don't mind?"

"Do you have any of those flavored packets that you pour into a water bottle?" he asked.

"Cherry, lemonade, and grape!" I replied.

I gave Walter just about all the supplies I had in my truck that day. Canned soup and a can opener, peaches, peanut butter, jelly packets, pita bread, Nutribars, water, toilet paper, paper towels, blankets, a portable propane heater, radio, and I cannot remember what else. I was driven to do what he would allow me to do to try to help. He graciously accepted and said these words as we parted company.

> "You're a good guy, Guy! I can tell that you love the Lord. You travel and minister to all those kids! God's gotta be pleased with you! Keep it up, my friend, keep it up."

On those words, we parted company. "God's gotta be pleased with me? GOD'S GOTTA BE PLEASED WITH ME?" The words rattled in my head for the next two days! God was not pleased with me that day. I let God down on that day. When I should have been the first person to approach this homeless man and offer assistance, I was the last. When I should have taken up Walter's cross and carried it for him, I was too busy worrying about my own.

> com-pas-sion: sympathetic consciousness of others' distress together with a desire to alleviate it (*Webster's Dictionary* 2013)

Having compassion for someone goes far beyond feeling sorry for them. It goes *way* beyond the behavior I exhibited that day in California. Walter did not receive compassion from me that day, he received judgment and condemnation. It was not until God looked at me and said, "Just who do you think you are, Guy? Are you a child of mine or not! You cannot have it both ways, dude. Now get out there and *earn* the words of that teacher I sent to encourage you! I am not going to allow *you* to make a liar out of *her!*"

Being compassionate means that we are unconditionally open to doing whatever it takes to serve the purpose God has for us. If it is to spend time with a homeless person, so be it. It is not our place to decide whether they are worthy or not. All too often we are approached with a decision that outsteps the boundary of our comfort zone. We make judgments like, "Oh, they are just going to spend the $5 I gave them on booze!" or "They are probably going to walk around the corner and get in their Lincoln Town Car!" It would serve us well to remember that it is not our concern what the receiver of our "gifts" does with the gift! Our responsibility is to answer the call that God places on our heart. God showed all of us more compassion than we can comprehend by dying on the cross for us. Show compassion in your life. We have much we can afford to share with others.

Principle 6 of the ARVIS Effect: Compassion
Let's Remember What Is Really Important!

> If your enemy is hungry, feed him; if he is thirsty, give him something to drink; for by so doing you will heap burning coals on his head. (Romans 12:20)

I have always liked this scripture because it has always defined how I treat those who are set on hurting me in some way. "Killing them with kindness" if you will. Let's examine this scripture a bit more closely as it relates to the story of Walter very closely. In most cases, we read this scripture and assume that it is speaking *to* us and not *about* us. In my case, I was the enemy who was having hot coals heaped on my head. In my predetermined judgment of Walter, I became his enemy, if you want to know the truth. I had never even met the man and had passed judgment on him.

However, in this case, Walter showed compassion to me in that he showed me kindness even when I was the apparent jerk! Even though he did not give me a thing, he heaped a ton of hot coals on my head by showing me my own dark underbelly.

Like I teach the kids in my school assembly programs, being nice to someone is easy when they are being nice to you! However, it is a true show of character to be nice to someone when they are being rude or ugly to you! I was a bully that day. Even though I did not push or hit Walter, I was the aggressor and he was the heaper of the hot coals.

Showing compassion to all who we come into contact with is a win-win situation. We exhibit the grace and understanding that Christ's example set for us. It softens our enemy and draws us closer to God. Compassion in the face of an adversary is the ultimate show of Christ's influence in our lives. I have always believed that we all mess up! Some of us mess up *huge*! It's not how much or how big we mess up that matters. It's how we *recover* from it that makes all the difference!

Show compassion to others. Someday you will want someone to show compassion to you.

8

BEYOND THE MAGIC

It's 2012 in a small rural town in Northeast Georgia. It's hot and thick outside. In the distance, the mountains are shining brightly on the horizon and the brilliant blue sky radiates behind a wall of white fluffy clouds. Smile, laughter, and everyday life are blooming. Flowers are filling the air with a sweet fragrance, and the clock ticks away. The sun is beginning to give way to the purples and pinks of the Georgia sunset. A number is dialed. There is no answer!

As we move beyond the initial five principles of the ARVIS Effect, we now venture into principles that enhance our daily lives in ways that we cannot possibly imagine. As illustrated throughout this book, my mother and father instilled a sense of self and a sense of purpose in my brother and I that has remained in our lives to this very day. In our life, things will come and go, and the changes of life tend to last in terms of seasons. Careers, dreams, aspirations, goals, setbacks, crises, and rewards ebb and flow like the tide of a great ocean.

When the trials of life would get to me at some point or another, my father always used ask me the same questions: "Is what is happening to you your fault?" and "Is there anything that you can do to change it?" or "Who can you call upon to fix your problems for you?" All these were in response to some life-altering "crisis" that I was facing at the time. He had an ability to take his situations and surroundings seriously while managing to not take himself too seriously. He knew that to worry about things that are simply beyond your control or your ability to change is a ridiculous waste of time.

When I was diagnosed with the brain tumor, my dad, while being very compassionate, said, "Can you do anything about it? Can you go in and remove it yourself? Is there anything more you can do that you are not already doing?" Of course, the answer to all three was no. So he followed those questions with this statement: "If there is nothing you can do to remove it yourself, and it occurred on its own, and you arc already doing everything you can do, the only thing you can *really* do is trust that God will handle it!" Very smart guy my dad!

I can remember many occasions growing up when I would see the look of concern on my dad's face. Something would happen at the shop or someone or something would be troubling him. The thing is, these facial expressions of concern or worry would only be short-lived. After just a few minutes, he was back to himself. What happened? Did he just blow off his problems? Did he ignore the situation and pretend that it never happened? Absolutely not! My father remembered who was in charge. He knew that he did not create the universe and that he was not the one who was in control. My father knew that worrying about things beyond your control is a lesson in futility.

My father had the inspiring ability to forgive truly, yet never forgetting the initial circumstances that brought about the forgiveness in the first place. You know the old saying "Forgive and forget" right? Let me ask you a question: How many of you reading these words have the ability to unconditionally forgive as well as unconditionally forget! The two are vastly different. I have always been the one who has a memory like an elephant—well, my wife may argue with me on that, but at least as far as those who have hurt me, I have a mind like a steel trap! When it comes to things like remembering to take out the trash, my mind is more like a steel window screen!

Question: "Is it possible to forgive without forgetting?" I know that as far as I am concerned, the forgetting part is more difficult than the forgiving part. I am going to lay all my cards out on the table here. I am an entertainer, an author, a lighting designer, entrepreneur, minister, and all-around decent guy (in my humble opinion). However, one thing that is not in that list is I am also a man who can hold on to a grudge like a prized pearl harvested from the depths of the deepest sea! I can forgive, sure! But forget? Forget it!

I told someone one time that I am slow to anger and am quick to forgive. They asked me, "Are you quick to forget too?" I thought about that for a moment and came to the shameful conclusion of "No...no, I am not quick to forget, if I forget at all!" Can we truly forgive and never forget? Yes! Forgiveness hinges on our ability to let go of the hurt. However, forgetting is not required. When we are hurt by another person's actions, we learn. We are growing in the spirit of the Lord. We are strengthened and sharpened by the fire of our particular circumstance. If we forget, we are always destined to repeat the same types of hurts and pain.

What is required, though, is the willingness and the ability to refrain from holding grudges and judging someone because of their past hurts or actions against us. The Bible has always been paraphrased as God casting our sins into the "sea of forgetfulness." Actually, the scripture reads, "He will again have compassion on us, and will subdue our iniquities. He will cast our sins into the depths of the sea" (Micah 7:19, NIV). God does not actually forget our sins.

He discounts our sins as invalid when we are saved by Jesus Christ. If we forgive someone yet hold them accountable every time we see them, we have not truly forgiven. We are a fraud if we never let go of the pain of what those who have hurt us did to be forgiven of in the first place! It's a hollow gesture. It's the very same as those who say "I am sorry" over and over and over while they continue to exhibit the behavior they are apologizing for. It's meaningless unless there is a real change in our hearts and is not solely dependent on their behavior. The same goes with forgiveness. If we "forgive" someone for doing us wrong and never let go of the pain of what they did, we are holding them to a standard of judgment that none of us can live up to. Forgetting is not important. What is important is unconditional forgiveness! We have a tendency to say, "Oh, I've forgiven you…" But have we really?

It's 2010, and I have recovered from my brain tumor operation and am beginning to reenter the workforce as a lighting designer in the Great Smoky Mountains. I am hired to work at a small magic show in the area and subsequently became close friends with the entertainer and his wife. He, his wife, myself, and my wife were the "fabulous four." *Inseparable* would be the term in this case. This man and I were collaborators professionally, and it was great! I ended up looking at this man as being closer to me than my own brother (at the time), and I thought I had finally found that "friend for life" type of situation.

He would consult me for creative ideas, and I him for performance ideas, and together we made the dynamic duo. We were unstoppable, and were willing to challenge all who would dare oppose us! Get the picture? We were arrogant a—s is what we were! We were so full of ourselves and amazed at our own awesomeness that we did not see anyone else or take anyone else's opinion, thoughts, or feelings into consideration. Little did I know, I was alienating some of those who were closest to me at the time.

Fast-forward a few years, and what do you have? In my particular case, I found out that I was nothing more than a source for ideas, and when my usefulness had been exhausted, I was cast aside like yesterday's garbage. To this day, I still do not know what I did or said to warrant such abandonment from the man I once thought of as my own brother. You want to talk about forgiveness? No way! Forgetting? Absolutely not! I sat and stewed on all the "What did I dos?" and the "How could hes!" for months— well, actually, years! I was not about to forgive nor was I about to forget! "I can't believe he would use me like this and then drop me like a hot potato with not so much as a single word!" was the thought that burned its way through my mind on a daily basis! It absolutely consumed me to the point it was all I could think about.

This all took place shortly after I met my then future wife, LaDonna, in a little park in Helen, Georgia. I was spending the weekends driving from Tennessee to Georgia to see her and to get to know her family when the thought occurred to me that I was allowing this man to occupy so much of my thought time that I was neglecting what was really important. I was allowing this man to control my emotions remotely! I was giving him far too much power over me, and it was then that God told me that I needed to forgive him. "Fine!" I said with a huff! "But I'll never forget what he did to me!" I dictated to the Lord. It was then that I had an "aha" moment that God had been trying to give me. "Forgetting is not required! What is required is not only forgiveness but letting go of the hurt and judgment of him!" God said very clearly.

This was the hardest thing I have ever had to do. Letting go of the judgment of his actions would prove to be very difficult. Every time I thought of him, I would get angry! God did not want me to forget. After all, I learned a valuable lesson from this experience. God wanted me to let go of the anger, judgment, and thoughts of egging his car if I ever saw him again!

Principle 7 of the ARVIS Effect: Forgiveness
We Do Not Need to Forget! We Need to Let Go!

> Brothers and sisters, I do not consider myself yet to
> have taken hold of it. But one thing I do: Forgetting
> what is behind and straining toward what is ahead.
> (Philippians 3:13, NIV)

Now it would appear that I just contradicted what I said above with the scripture I just used. To some, letting go of the hurt would be considered as forgetting. If that works for you, go with it. However, for me, I make the distinction between forgetting and letting go of the pain.

God's desire for us is that we do not sin at all. However, since we do sin, every day, God takes the sins of those who believe in His son and live (as best they can) by the teachings and example Jesus set for us and throw them as far as the "East is from the West" (Psalm 103:12). God does not forget about the sin, He simply no longer cares about them! We are forgiven—truly!

How can this example apply to us? How can we use this to our benefit? Simple. Remember that holding grudges serves no one. It will not affect the person who hurt us in the slightest. They could truly care less, and they are going about their business as if it never happened. Holding a grudge hurts only one person—us! Bitterness, anger, and resentment can infiltrate our lives simply by dwelling on the hurt. Forgive the person for what they did to you. It's okay not to forget it! This way, we will recognize when someone is repeating the same type of hurt. However, it is a *must* that we let go of the ill effects of that hurt. That is the true meaning of forgiveness.

9

VISITING BROOKLYN

*December, 2015. The words "Friends are God's way of tak-
ing care of us" are shining brightly from a 5x5 plaque on the
wall. Clothes, boots, and shoeboxes are scattered around the floor
displaying sharp contrast to the tan carpet. Blue jeans with a
camel colored belt lay on the floor just where she left them when
she changed clothes. Trophies on display, cheerleading memora-
bilia, and a small yellow megaphone with the initials S.H.S.
sit atop a white bookshelf. An unmade bed with white rails and
giraffe pattern pillowcases match the small picture of a giraffe
and giraffe figurine located across the room. A bottle of "Be
Enchanted" body spray sits on top of a black boom box that plays
her favorite music. On the wall above the bed is one of my all
time favorite scriptures. "I can do all things through Christ who
strengthens me." This is the typical room of almost any 14 year
old girl in America! An organized "mess" is what anyone would*

expect to find in the room of a beautiful young girl with a smile that would light up even the darkest of places. There is only one thing that doesn't belong… the cardboard box sitting at the foot of the bed.

The year is 1983 and it's a typical school year in Arlington Texas. I was a sophomore and I, like everyone else, was trying to figure out this whole new world of a brand new school, brand new people, and brand new rules. The school had recently been built and we were the first students to ever grace the hallways of the shiny new flagship of the Arlington Independent School District. The place was alive with energy as we all negotiated for our positions in the physical school, but also for our positions in the social dynamic that is inherent in any school. Students who knew each other from years past were mixed in with students who were brand new to the area. Students who had relationships already formed were thrust into new relationships with total strangers. This… was HIGH SCHOOL!

As I have mentioned in previous chapters, I was removed from the public school system at a pretty young age and placed in a small (very small) private Christian school. The social pool of position and status was tiny so it was easy for me to carve out a niche for myself. I was one of the most popular kids in my school at the time. I was top dog of the 9th grade!! Of course… there were only 16 kids in the entire

9th grade! I was a fish who was larger than life in the puddle of social opportunity that was my little private school.

Because my school did not offer grades higher than 9th, I was forced to go to a public high school. Overnight my world expanded from 16 students in my 9th grade class to over 500 students in my 10th grade class! I was totally lost, alone, and afraid.

As the school year progressed, most were able to find their place and settle in their routines. They began to build their lives as high school students as they gained friends, experiences and something of a social schedule. Remember, in 1983 there were no cell phones, Facebook or Instagram. We had to communicate the old fashioned way... Face to Face! Ugh!

My mother and father always taught me the value of eye contact and clear open communication with anyone you wish to speak with. Telling the truth, being kind (even when you don't want to be) and speaking through a smile were the staples on which I was raised. I was the type of teenager who cared what people thought about me and I wanted to try to please everyone. I would smile and say "Hi" in an effort to win friends and to try to hold on to the popularity that I had enjoyed only a year prior. Nothing worked.

As I sat in the background observing the different clicks and how they operated, I tried to decipher the codes that were obviously unspoken yet were clearly understood by the members of those clicks. At my school, as with any high school, we had the jocks, cheerleaders, football players (they were in a group all their own), drama kids, nerds, geeks, and just about any other stereotype you can imagine. Where did I fit in?

To make a long story short, I fit in nowhere. I was one of the unclassified, who were part of the nameless few who wandered the halls looking for somewhere to belong. Not being overly athletic, I did not really fit with the jock crowd. I was not overly interested in academics so I did not gel with the really smart kids. I did enjoy drama but since I was not a good actor, I remained behind the scenes delegated to the "crew", which was not the sought after place in the drama club. I knew everyone yet no one knew me. I knew their names and they had no clue that I existed, nor did they care to find out. "Oh your that guy... aren't you?" was the standard greeting I received on a daily basis.

Before the days of "anti-bullying" movements and things like cyber-bullying we had the old fashioned bullying of the "glory" days! None of this hiding behind our phones while taking anonymous jabs at someone we don't like. There was no texting, sexting, or "Snap Chatting". There were no means to send mean-spirited pictures to the entire school before the bell rings.

There was no such thing as Facebook or any other of the hundreds of social media sites that would allow a bully to hide behind the anonymity of a computer screen. No. In those days, bullying was up close and very personal. A bully had to be committed to his or her craft in order to be a success. They had to be willing to be accountable for their actions because it was face to face or not at all.

Of the hundreds of instances where I encountered bullies that humiliated, intimidated, and belittled me, I choose to share one instance as it clearly ties in to the purpose of this chapter.

As I have lived my life as an adult and through my studies of psychology, human behavior and why we do the things we do, I have discovered a phenomenon that I did not recognize as a young teenager. I am speaking about the *pack* mentality. I never understood why someone, who I thought was my friend, would turn against me when other people were around. This always confused me and left deep scars as only moments before we would be laughing and joking around with each other. It was not until others joined in the conversation that things would turn ugly.

During this particular incident, I was a trainer for the football team. Trainers were the students that would assist the Head Trainer (medical guy) with minor injuries that would occur during a football game. We had just won the playoff game and everyone was on cloud nine and were hooping and hollering on the busses on the way back home. Everyone on my bus hatched a plan to get together at Mr.

Jim's pizza once we got back home. Everyone was excited about the win and wanted to celebrate with a victory pizza at "Jim's!" The invites were going around the bus, and I wondered if they would make it all the way up to where I was sitting. It did! "Hey you want to come with us?" the QUARTERBACK shouted at me!! I was thrilled! I had never been included in something like this before! I WAS IN!! I WAS PART OF THE GROUP!! YES!!! I eagerly replied (but with a calm exterior of course) "Sure!" I had to play it cool you know! I couldn't be too excited or I would look like a loser! On the inside though, I was exploding with joy at being included. Finally I was part of the team that went everywhere and did everything together.

We arrived back at the school and once everyone had put their stuff away and had gotten cleaned up the QB said "Ok... we will see everyone at Jim's in half an hour!" "Man oh man this is going to be awesome" I thought to myself. "The playoff champions, the winning team, is going to celebrate and I am going with them!" These were the thoughts that danced through my head like the song "It's a small world" after having taken a ride on the famous attraction at Disney World. I WAS STOKED!

Half an hour later I pulled into the Mr. Jim's parking lot. There were not a lot of cars there yet so I looked in the windows and saw the QB, a couple of the cheerleaders and a few of the other players on the team. I figured that everyone had not yet arrived so I went inside and approached the "cool" group, of which I was now a part! "Hey!!! You're here!" they shouted. They had smiles on their faces and were patting me on the back. I was glowing. I had finally made it. I was in!

"Where is everyone?" I asked. "They are not coming" one of them said. "Their not coming? Why?" I asked. "Because no one wants to hang out with a loser like you!" The group sang those words in unison as they patted me on the back and laughed in my face while they walked out the door.

I was left standing there among a crowd of strangers, alone and humiliated. Everything that had been said on the bus was for my benefit. An orchestrated plan with one purpose in mind… to humiliate and belittle someone who wanted nothing more than to be a part of their "family". I found out later that everyone did get together, they just did not tell me where real location was. I do not tell this story to generate sympathy as this happened many years ago. I tell you this story because the pain of that night stays with me to this day. Wanting to belong, fit in, be a part of something bigger than ourselves, is normal. The pain and humiliation of being the center of an elaborate plan designed to make you feel small and inadequate never goes away.

In the days following I remember speaking to my Father about what had happened to me. I begged him not to tell my Mother as I knew that it would break her heart and I did not want her to worry about me. So, I went to my dad and said "Dad, can I tell you something?" He said "Why sure!! You know you can tell me anything son!" So I proceeded to tell him what had happened and how I was feeling about those people, as well as, myself. I will never forget what he said to me.

He said… "Son, I have been where you are. I can see in your eyes the hurt and the anger that you feel towards those people. I know your embarrassed and that you don't really know what to do" he said. "I know you want to be a part of that group but let me ask you this… "Would you ever want to do to someone else what they did to you?" "NO!!!" I said with a shout. My Father, who had wisdom that seems to have been lost in this current generation, then said the words that would become the foundation on which I try my best to incorporate into my relationships.

He said "Even though you were humiliated and left standing there alone and embarrassed, you are the winner here!" "What? How so?" I asked. "I want you to REMEMBER what it felt like to have that done to you. Don't worry about them. You worry about the way YOU treat other people. Use this as a lesson in what NOT to do! Treat people the exact opposite of how they treated you!" "If you can do that son… you will be a winner all of your life no matter what everyone else is doing." Wise man my dad!

I have never shared that story with anyone, other than my Father, until the writing of these words. My family, including my mother, brother, wife and children will find out about this story when they read this book for the first time. So why did I decide to share the pain of this story now? Three words... Brooklyn Nicole Howard.

March 11th, 2014 approximately 6 PM. In a quaint little town in Arkansas, a man is wrapping up an afternoon of fishing. After enjoying one of his favorite ways to relax, his cell phone rings. A familiar voice on the other end of the line say's "Wherever you are, whatever you are doing, stop now and get home!" "What's going on?" he asks. "Just get home!" The voice says. He hangs up the phone and starts the journey towards the house. His mind is racing and every thought you can imagine is screaming around in his head. Foot on the accelerator, this turn, that turn, traffic lights and stop signs all turning into a blur as he anguishes over the unknown. The phone rings again. A different, yet familiar, voice says "What's this I hear about Brooke shooting herself?" The world stopped spinning upon hearing those eight words.

March 23rd, 2014 early afternoon. Knoxville Tennessee. I am sitting in my hypnotherapy office with a woman who had buried her daughter 13 days prior. Overcome with grief, guilt, loss, and despair she has reached out to me for some sort of relief from her suffering. "God, I do not know what to say to this woman who has suffered so much. What do I say to her? How do I help her?" "You brought her to me for a reason Lord, teach me what to say. Show me what to do" This was my prayer while the details of her story were unfolding before my ears. During this session is when I learned about a beautiful, vibrant, walking smile named Brooklyn "Brooke" Nicole Howard.

With the permission of her family, I am going to tell the story of a girl who has impacted my life in an unexpected way. I did not know this girl personally, yet after having been involved with her family, so soon after her passing, I feel as though I have a personal connection with this amazing young lady. I am going to speak about her in the present tense because she is and will always remain an active part in the lives of those who knew and loved her.

Brooke is a 14 year old girl who lives in a small town, deep in the heart of Arkansas. She is a young lady that carries with her a smile that is a never-ending blessing. A cheerleader, athlete, beauty queen, and avid hunter, Brooke is the poster child for the "All American Girl". The youngest of three children, Brooke is an inspiration to mother Debbie, father Steve, her brother Hunter as well as her big sister Chelsea. She is the picture of youth and is overflowing with an eagerness to help. Brooke is a really "cool" kid to put it simply.

Brooke is a good student and has lots to offer anyone who comes across her path. She has lots of friends and is involved in many sports and activities at school. She is a great hunter who proudly displays her successes on the trophy wall. She has a young romance going and seems to be on top of the world. This young lady has an energetic exterior, but unknown to others, that energetic exterior is masking an interior pain. The exact details that lead up to the events that took place on March 11th, 2014, are known only to Brooke. However, as time has passed, details have become apparent. Brooke was the victim of bullying.

I recently traveled to Brooke's home to meet with her family in order to gain some insight into what happened and more importantly… why? As I sat with the family, I was struck by their open communication and sense of purpose around the loss of their daughter and younger sister. They were very clear in their intentions to bring forth good from the tragedy of their loss. It is not their intent, nor is it mine, to point fingers or to place blame on any one person, however, it is our intent to shine a spotlight on the seriousness of bullying, in any form. Bullying is not cool. Bullying is not funny. Bullying someone else is not going to make you feel better. Bullying is painful. Bullying is sad. Bullying is deadly! "Brooke made a decision in the heat of the moment" her father said. "She let the pain of the bullies influence her thoughts and she acted on it" he continued. The message here is not to place blame, the message here is to drive home the seriousness and the devastating effects that bullying can have on any family.

The connection that I personally have with Brooke is not that she was beat up by a bully… she wasn't. Brooke was a victim of the exact same kind of bullying that I was subjected too, rejection by people she thought were her friends. Things like eye rolls, sighs, hidden laughter, whispers, demeaning comments, and dismissive gestures are just as powerful and painful as a punch in the gut. In fact, they are more painful than just being direct about it. Rejection is one of the most widely used and most painful forms of bullying that there is. Why? Because it's easier. Confronting or bullying someone physically may just get you bullied right back. But social rejection, abandonment, controlling, being ostracized and cyber-bullying is much more effective and easier to hide behind.

The manipulation, and the pack mentality that I experienced, that night at the pizza place, is the same form of bullying that lead Brooke to take her own life on March 11th, 2014. A true friend is a true friend regardless of who's around. A boyfriend or girlfriend is the one who should treat you the best, not the worst. In my case, those who I thought were my friends were only my friends when no one was looking. When others were around, they banded together to belittle, mock and make fun. The same thing happened to Brooke.

During our conversation I asked the family for a specific example of the bullying that Brooke experienced. Debbie told me of an incident that took place about a month before Brooke passed away. On the surface this incident seemed fairly innocent, however, when told in the context of the monumental effect that Brooke's continual exposure had, as well as similar situations have had on hundreds of students across the country, it wasn't innocent at all.

We were sitting in the family room that was adorned with pictures, hunting trophies, a pellet burning fireplace, and a warm, welcoming feeling of love and family. Debbie and I were sitting on the couch, Brooke's father (Steve) sat in a chair to my left, and Brooke's brother (Hunter) and sister (Chelsea) sat across from us on another couch. This was a very emotional part of our visit as laughter, tears and memories flooded the room. As I held on to a picture of Brooke, Debbie told me of a time when Brooke had mentioned that one of her friends in school approached her and asked *"Hey Brooke what's wrong?"* (The smile that usually announced Brooke's presence was missing on that day.) Brooke told her mother that she replied to the friend *"Well, I am just a little tired of the way you guys roll your eyes, whisper, and laugh at me every time I say or do something!"* Brooke then told her mom what the friend said in response. "*I guess we can stop. We've been doing it for a while now!*" Debbie said how she gave her daughter the motherly advice that one would expect, "*Well just remember to always be as kind as you can sweetheart!*" Brooke's response to this advice is what stood out to me in this conversation. "*I always am mom... I always am.*"

Brooke's sweet spirit and sensitive nature was firmly rooted by her parents and the example they had always set for her. The scripture "For whatever you wish that others would do to you, do also to them." (Matthew 7:12) was more than just a Sunday school lesson for Brooke, it was her way of life. Even as her mother was expressing her desire to come to her daughter's defense, it was more important to Brooke that she remain true to the values she held so dear. Being kind, keeping the peace, being a true friend regardless if it was reciprocated, was always more important to Brooke than her own defense.

To prevent further pain for the family, I will not disclose further details surrounding Brooke's death. I will however disclose that her bullying was very real, very painful and it lead to her mother having to perform CPR on, say goodbye too, and bury her daughter as a result. Her father is the man I mentioned earlier, who was finishing up a day of fishing. The news of "something's wrong" traveled quickly to Brooke's brother and sister as they were all grasping to make sense of it all. They were all looking for the answer to a single question. Why? The Howard family said "Goodbye" to their daughter, sister, and best friend on that day. Is bullying really worth the price we all pay? Is it?

As the stories of the events that occured were told, I was immersed into the scene of the tragedy that unfolded in their lives. Moments of that day were shared. Tears were shed. I saw a family who has strengthened their bond as a result of a single decision made in an instant. What stood out the most, what shouted louder than any words was their strength, their unity, and their desire to see good come from the senseless loss of such an amazing life. In every member of Brooke's family I saw a clear sense of purpose. A clear desire to spread the message that bullying is real. Bullying is serious and painful, and bullying has life changing consequences.

Toward the end of the visit, I was invited into Brooke's bedroom, which has remained unchanged and undisturbed since that horrible day in 2014. (I am writing this chapter on New Years Eve 2015, so it's been almost two years since that day) As I entered the room, I could feel the energy that Brooke left behind. A messy, unmade bed that was peppered with the patterns of giraffe skin pillowcases. Wadded up clothes and messy covers, made it feel as though she had just gotten out of bed. There were clothes on the floor strewn about as if she had just changed from one outfit to the next. Pictures of her and her mom on the dresser were intermingled with candlesticks and pottery. There were trophies everywhere! From softball to cheerleading to who knows what, she was clearly an accomplished young lady. There was a small deer antler sitting on the dresser just above the Mossy Oak hunting boots proudly displayed outside her closet door. Crosses and scriptures dotted her wall's as did the saying mentioned previously that emphasized the importance of "Friends".

This was the stereotypical room of a 14 year old girl with a life full of adventure, life full of love, and a life full of experiences waiting ahead of her. As also mentioned previously, there was one thing that did not belong in her room. This thing does not belong in anyone's room... ever. It was a cardboard box on the foot of her bed with a case file number written on the side. The life of a young lady had been classified, by the police department, into an eight-digit number. This box contains the blood soaked clothes that Brooke was wearing that day. It also contains the blood stained gun that she used to end the pain she hid so well. This box remained at the police station from March 11th, 2014 until just a few months ago. It has yet to be opened.

One other item contained in the box is a single piece of paper that simply reads...

"This had nothing to do with anyone, it was my choice. I am so blessed that I had a great family like yall. I love yall SO much! I will see yall again another day! Thanks for always being there for me! Yall mean everything to me. Everything has been so stressful lately. Mom and Chelsea make sure I look good and thanks for always being there. Dad and Hunter I guess yall can add a little camo. Thanks for always taking me hunting. Thank yall for making me the girl I wa am. I LOVE YALL! I will have the time of my life in heaven with God"—Brooke

After our visit, hugs were exchanged as we shared hopeful optimism that somehow the story of Brooklyn Nicole Howard could be told. I told the family I had no idea of how God would move or in what form He would have me share what had come to rest so heavily on my heart. We parted ways and I started my journey back to the hotel. Halfway there, I was overcome with emotion and had to pull the car to the side of the road. As I reviewed the videos and pictures that I had been given, the impact that this girl has had on me is unexplainable.

The next morning, as I headed out of town, I made a detour. I traveled a few miles out of my way and ended up at a peaceful little cemetery located just out of town. The family had shown me a picture, and after looking through the entire place I finally found her. On a cold morning in December, I found myself sitting on a metal bench with the initials BNH engraved on the back. On the ground before me were flowers, Christmas packages, and a white cross that simply said Brooke. I sat there for about an hour and just prayed that God would continue to comfort the family, give me direction and that He would let Brooke know that there is a man that is looking forward to meeting her one day.

> re-mem-ber: To have or keep an image or idea in your mind of (something or someone from the past): To think of (someone or something from the past) again. *(Miriam Webster, 2013)*

Principle 8 Of The ARVIS Effect: Remembering Let Us Not Forget That Which Teaches Us

> "But the Helper, the Holy Spirit, whom the Father will send in My name. He will teach you all things, and bring to your remembrance all that is said to you." (John 14:25 NIV)

I chose to include this chapter because along with the other principles outlined in this book, they will not serve us well if we do not *remember* where it was that we come from. If we forget what it was like to have been the victim of a bully, we will surely become a bully ourselves. The purpose of this chapter is also to ask you, the reader, to remember how important it is to forgive.

> "Forgiveness is the fragrance that the violet sheds upon the heel that has crushed it."
>
> —Mark Twain

To forgive someone for their transgressions against us does not serve to benefit them. Rather, forgiveness serves to benefits us. As Dr. Wayne Dyer so elegantly put it.

> "It's not the snake bite that kills the victim. No one has ever died from a snake bite… it's just a bite!"
> "What kills you is the venom that courses through your veins after the bite takes place."

Just as the snakes venom eventually kills it's prey, so does bitterness and resentment kill the person who refuses to forgive. Just as I have forgiven those who treated me wrong, and the Howard family has forgiven those who treated their beautiful daughter with disregard and cruelty, my hope is that you will forgive those who have treated you wrong as well.

The testimony that I gave in this chapter is a very personal and very painful part of my history. As a 48 year old professional entertainer, who has traveled all over the world, those around me do not realize that in some ways, I am still that 16 year old, humiliated kid, standing alone in the middle of a crowd. I do not dwell on those memories now as I have moved on, and have enjoyed much success in my life. However, the effects of those memories are still present and have an impact on my life, when I let them. More than negative now, those memories serve as a reminder that I am to treat people the way I always wanted to be treated when I was a kid. To be kind, gentle, positive, and uplifting to all that I come into contact with.

Visitng Brooklyn in her home and becoming familiar with the person and the memory of such an amazing young lady has reminded me, in a very powerful way, that people need kindness in their life. Something as simple as a smile given to replace an "eye roll" can literally save someone's life. A warm welcome, firm handshake and a sincere "How are you?" can change the course of someone who may be headed down the wrong path.

When we think of bullying, we traditionally think of physical bullying, a bigger kid pushing around a smaller one. Brooke, however, faced a much more sinister and harder to recognize form of bullying... Relational bullying. Relational bullying takes the form of friends turning against friends because of peer pressure. Young boys and girls trying to dominate and control the person they "care" about.

In my travels across the county, I have witnessed every form of bullying imaginable. From young ladies turning on their friends to get attention or a laugh, to young men acting out because they think it's "cool". I have seen countless young people try to emulate what they have seen on television, movies, or real life, by trying to control the thoughts and actions of the one they say they love. They try to dictate whom their significant other speaks too, rides with, communicates with, what they do, and who they interact with. That's not a friend, girlfriend or boyfriend. That's a piece of property.

During couples counseling, I will ask the couple individually.

"Mary, who is your best friend?" Mary says… *"Susan"* Then I ask *"Mary, how long would you and Susan be best friends if she tried to control who you spoke too, rode with, interacted with, what you did, where you go, who you go with, never listened to you, discounted you, laughed at you, and mocked you?"* Mary say's *"NOT LONG I CAN TELL YOU THAT!!!"* Then I say this to Mary, and I am saying it to you…

"Tell me, if you would not put up with that type of behavior from a friend, why then would you put up with it from someone who says they LOVE you and that you mean EVERYTHING

to them?" "Should they not be held to a higher standard than that of a friend?"

As one half of the relationship, we have the right and the responsibility to hold the other half to a *higher* standard, not give them countless passes. We tend to let those who are supposed to *love* us get away with *far* more than we would from those who *like* us. Why is that? It's simply because we hope they will change and will somehow become the person we hope they could be. This rarely happens. We have gotten it completely backwards. We do not accept bad behavior from friends, yet we allow those who claim to cherish us get away with things that are unimaginable.

Ladies, I would like to encourage you to stop and take a deep breath before you make a decision about your relationships or whom you get involved with. Before you decide to join in the humiliation of another person, in order to gain popularity, a laugh, or to look cool, look first into the mirror and ask "What if that were me?" Before you decide to let a guy who says he "loves" (or even likes) you control and dominate you, ask yourself "Does he *really* care for me when he apparently doesn't even trust me?" Brooke, like so many young ladies before and after her, became the victim of a flawed thought. The thought or belief that *your* needs are somehow less important than *his* wants, is a dangerous road to travel. If the person I just described is you? Hold out for a partner that values you as the creation God made you to be.

Guy's, here is what being a real man truly means. Being a man is not being mean, rude, or disrespectful. Being a man means that you are humble, and that you take what you know and put it to positive use. Being a man does not mean that you have to be in control. Constantly trying to be in control is a sign of weakness, not a sign of strength. When it comes to the woman in your life, if you truly do care for her, you will not try to impose your will upon her! You will support her. You will empower her. You will be her partner, not her captor. You will cherish her and will put her above yourself. You will put what *she needs* above what *you want.* True love is not getting your way. *True love is paving the way.* True love is walking side by side, hand in hand. Love is never dictating. Love is never demanding. Love never uses guilt. Love never shouts, and Love is never selfish.

If you are in a friendship that leaves you with negative feelings? CHANGE YOUR FRIENDS! If you are in a relationship that leaves you sad, questioning, alone, or depressed? CHANGE YOUR RELATIONSHIP! You are in control of you! You have the right and the responsibility to make the change necessary to ensure that your needs are being met.

Please, before you decide to make an impulsive decision, or find a permanent solution to a temporary problem, *TALK TO SOMEONE!*

By remembering what it was like when we were on the receiving end of a bully's heart can help us steer clear of spreading the virus that is bullying. I can speak from experience, and I believe that I can honestly speak for Brooke when I say… Any form of bullying, direct or indirect, leaves deep scars that can last a lifetime. Do the right thing, be kind and remember that no matter how innocent you may think your bullying is, the hurt and the lasting effects are real and powerful.

Before I left Brooke's grave I used my finger and wrote this line in the dirt. "I will tell your story." It is my hope that I have done her justice.

Remembering Brooklyn Nicole Howard is something that I will do for the rest of my life. She made an indelible mark on the lives of those she touched. This fact was vivid and clear at Brooke's funeral. The line to attend the service extended out of the building, the service was packed with hundreds of young men and women who, one after another, told the family *"Brooke was the only person at school who ever took the time to smile or to speak to me in the hallway."*

Brooke was a beautiful, vibrant, smiling teenager who made a permanent decision based on temporary circumstances. Her pain was real. Her impact will be felt forever.

For Brooke.

A memorial scholarship has been set up in Brooke's name as well as an Anti-Bullying program that will soon be traveling the country. For more information on the scholarship or for information on bringing the assembly to your school, please visit www.visitingbrooklyn.org

Postscript

As the flow of this book was coming to an end, I became entrenched in the thought that something was missing. I just could not find the words to complete this work. Everything flowed as God placed the words for this book in my heart. Then it just stopped. I could not continue. I had no more words. I learned a long time ago that things such as the words in this book cannot be forced. With deadlines looming, emails from the publisher coming in, I had nothing new to offer. The inspiration I had felt during the writing of this book simply dried up.

I prayed that God would give me the words to finish this book. Nothing came. Days turned into weeks and my frustration mounted. Then one afternoon God gave me the answer, Brooke Howard. God placed her story on my heart and the result is the words written in this chapter, but more importantly, the relationships formed with her family. What wonderful people and a true inspiration they are.

This is the reason that this chapter was written after the final chapter of this book. Chapters 1–8 came first. Then chapter 10. Chapter 9 did not come until New Years Eve 2015… tonight.

I am including this short note because the title of the final chapter is "The Gift of Goodbye". Not only is that title fitting for myself and my family, but now for the Howard family as well. In March of 2014 they said goodbye to their loved one. Six months later, I said goodbye to mine.

God Bless you Steve, Debbie, Chelsea, and Hunter.

10

THE GIFT OF GOOD-BYE

It's crisp outside. The smell of fire burning in the fireplaces once again fills the air. Everyone is sleeping, and I remain awake listening to the tick-tock of the clock. Minute by minute the time draws near. The soft purr of the laptop fan comforts as emotions well up inside.

I thought it fitting to conclude this book tonight. What is tonight? Tonight marks the first anniversary of the prayer when I asked God to take my father home. September 21, 2015, at 12:33 AM. Exactly one year ago tonight, I was sitting in my father's room and was holding his hand. Listening to him breathe, I was saying good-bye to my hero, the man who had served as an example for me for forty-seven years. Prayers had been said, tears had been shed, and the thoughts and emotions of the situation were running rampant through my head.

This book is written as a tribute to my father, yes…but more importantly, it is written to be a guide for all who read it. It was not written by a scholar or a politician or a reverend. It was written by an ordinary man who lost his extraordinary father. The reason I felt that this book must be written was because my father had a set of principles that he lived by. Those principles were simple: Treat people the way you want to be treated. Love God and try as best you can to live the way God wants us to live. Forgive others and just let it go. These are yet a few of the life lessons that I learned by having Arvis Gene Smith as my father.

A year ago, I was embarking on a journey for which I had no map. Like so many before me, my destination was unique to me. Only I could go on my journey and only I could glean the lessons to be learned from my father's life. In the year following my father's death, many things happened in my life. It's been a year of growth, maturing in the spirit, and a sense of calling on my life.

God has been working with me this year. He's been showing me many areas that I need to improve in, and a few where He is proud of my accomplishments. It has been four months since I last wrote a word in this book. I hit the writer's block that so many authors fear. I hit it dead-on like a brick wall.

Tonight, as I worked on the laptop finishing a test for school, I was also waiting for 4:00 AM to come. I do not know why really…I just felt it proper to remember a year ago in my own way. Yet…while waiting, the words for the final few chapters of this book came to mind. Not wanting to ramble on, I feel that it would be a fitting close to this book to say a few simple words directly to the reader of this book.

You may agree with the things I've said, or you may not. You may identify with my story, and you may not. One thing remains constant: If you are currently at a point in your life where God is talking to you, if He is moving in your life in some way, then smile. The creator of the universe took time out of his schedule a long time ago to create you. He gave you your personality, your likes, dislikes, emotions, sense of humor, looks, and so much more. He knows you inside and out, and He loves His creation.

Forty-eight years ago on May 18, 1967, God gave me to my mother and father. They taught me well, and for that, I will be eternally grateful. A year ago today, I said good-bye to my father because God decided it was time to take him home. What my father left me was a legacy of knowledge, wisdom, and caring. A guide if you will. There are many guides out there today! Guides on how to get rich! How to buy a house! How to get a job! How to get a mate! Just about anything you want to do, you can find a guide for.

One thing struck me as I was going over memories of my father. The guide that my father left me was not a guide to get rich or any of those things that I mentioned. My dad left me a guide that shows how to be fulfilled no matter who you are or what stage of life you are in.

Think about it for a moment. Have you ever known anyone who had more money than they could ever spend yet were miserable? Have you ever known anyone who had everything *you* ever wanted yet were unhappy all the time? Have you ever seen someone who had more, did more, got more, made more, spent more, and wanted more—yet had less than you? I have.

The founding principles of the ARVIS Effect are simple. By living your life by being *a*ccountable, *r*espectful, *v*igilant, as an *i*nspiration to others, and in the *s*ervice of others, you can be on top of life no matter what kind of house you live in. By living your life according to the ARVIS Effect, happiness and fulfillment is not dependent on money or status. It makes no difference what kind of car you drive or clothes you wear.

The ARVIS principle has an effect on everyone no matter where they are. It's an effect that will draw you closer to God and will help you learn to listen for God's voice in your life. I do not know about you, but sometimes it's hard to hear God's voice over all the noise that Satan shouts at us. We often lose our ability to see and hear what is really important—God.

At this time in our country, we are facing unprecedented changes in attitude, tolerance, and ignorance of God and Christianity. The influence of God in this country is trying to be discounted and negated at every turn. If there were ever a time to listen for the voice of God, it's now. It is my sincerest hope that you will see the spirit in which this book was written. It's not intended to be a documentary about Arvis Gene Smith. Nor is it meant to be a book of moments of my life. It was written with the hopes that it will speak to you wherever you are in your life—that perhaps one of the principles outlined here will speak to you in some way.

A year ago today, God gave me the gift of good-bye. He allowed me to spend forty-seven years with my father, and when it came time to say good-bye, although it was said through tears, I know in my heart that my dad and I had no unfinished business. That he and I shared a relationship that is not very common among fathers and sons. On September 22, 2014, at 4:00 AM, God gave the gift of good-bye to my entire family. We were comforted by His spirit and consoled by His wisdom.

Wisdom is something that my father passed on to me, and I intend to pass it on to my kids. The principles of the ARVIS Effect will live on in my family. It is my sincerest hope that it lives on in yours as well.

As I have stated many times throughout this book. I am not a scholar, religious leader, scientist, politician, sports hero, or first responder. I am a simple entertainer whom you have never heard of who performs in Gatlinburg, Tennessee, and lives in Cleveland, Georgia. Writing a book was not something that I ever thought would be on my radar, yet here we are. Even though I am not any of those things listed above, what I am, however, is a man who loves the Lord. I mess up every day, yet I try as hard as I can to recognize my mistakes and to hear the counsel that God gives me.

A final thought. Words in a book must come to an end at some point. Images on the movie screen must go dark eventually. Tall tales and memories fade over time as does hurt and pain as the clock ticks away. What will never fade, however, is the love of Jesus Christ and His plan for our life. Jesus speaks to us all in the unique way that only you and He know. He does not shout from the mountaintops, he whispers gently to your heart. Will you listen? Will you respond?

I pray that you do.

I thought it fitting to close with the words of a man whose music I grew up listening to. He has since faded into oblivion, yet to me, his music ministers to me in a way I never thought possible. His name is Gary Dunham, and he wrote a song that I would like to share with you as the final thought of this book. It is my hope that the words of this song adequately convey the heart in which this book was written.

To Arvis Gene Smith, I love you, Dad! You taught me well. You taught me well!

The Lord Is Greater
(G. Dunham and R. Dunham, *Happy Family*,
New Pax Records, NP33086, 1980)

Oh, dear brothers and sisters
I hope that I can help
By sharing what God's showing me
I hope you see yourself
Maybe you feel that one too many times
You've walked away
But His love is everlasting
And the price completely paid

(Chorus)

God is greater than our failures
Greater than our sin
And greater is His love for us
Than all our love for Him
His light is brighter than the brightest ray

Of hope we can conceive
Praise our God, and Lord is greater
Than even believers believe

It's hard just to imagine
This love that's from the Lord
The one who gave so freely
What we could not afford
And I don't think we can understand
The depth of what was done
The freedom and forgiveness
That He gives us in His Son

Repeat Chorus

Dear child, He knows you love Him
He sees beyond your tears
You're His despite the weakness
You're His despite the fears
And we can only praise Him
For His love for you and me
He has healed the brokenhearted
He has set the captive free

Repeat Chorus

About the Cover

The picture used on the cover of this book was taken back in 2011. I was on the beach in North Carolina while performing one of my Scream N' Shout assemblies. I was between events when I decided to go to the beach for some inspiration. While there, I saw more starfish than I had ever seen before. There were hundreds of them in a very confined space. When I approached them, I was reminded of a story about the man on the beach.

> One early morning, a man was going for his daily run on the beach just as the sunlight began to break the darkness over the horizon. As he ran, listening to his favorite music, he saw something strange way off in the distance. *What is that?* he thought to himself as he witnessed someone acting and moving very strangely on the beach. The closer he got to this person, he could tell that it was a man who appeared to be dancing.

As he approached the man, he began to see that this man was not dancing; rather, he was picking something up and throwing it back into the ocean. Once the runner got close enough to see clearly, he could see that this man was throwing starfish into the ocean.

The runner asked the man, "Excuse me, sir, but might I ask what it is that you are doing?"

The man replied, "I am throwing these starfish back into the water so they won't die!"

The runner surveyed the beach around them and saw thousands upon thousands of starfish for as far as the eye could see!

The runner said to the man, "You are crazy! There are so many starfish on this beach, there is no way you can get to them all! There is no way what you are doing will make any kind of a difference!"

The man was holding a starfish in his hand, and as he looked at it, he held it out toward the runner and said these words: "Maybe I can't make a difference to all of these star fish! But I sure can make a difference to *this* one!"

—(L. Eiseley, "The Starfish Thrower," 1969)

The picture on the cover of this book is of my hand holding a starfish. At the time, I just snapped the picture because I thought it was a good shot and it reminded me of that story. It was not until the writing of this book that I realized what the true meaning of the picture was. The five points of the starfish are the five principles of the ARVIS Effect. Each one is unique unto itself, yet they all rely on each other to make the starfish (the ARVIS Effect) complete. It sits atop my hand because, just like in life, the principles that we choose to live by are supported (or not supported) by the decisions that *we* make. Like the hand in the picture, choosing to support the five, very important, yet fragile, elements of the starfish, we make a choice to support (or not) the very fragile, yet crucial, principles that we choose to live our life by.

I chose to support the starfish and to throw it back into the life-sustaining water from which it came. I'm sure the starfish did not choose to end up stranded on the beach, struggling to survive. However, the ebb and flow of the tide, and the challenges it brings, washed the starfish ashore. Sound familiar? We don't usually choose to strand ourselves on the beaches of our life, causing us to struggle to maintain life. Yet the grind of that very life often causes us to wind up in a deserted place wondering how (and if) we will survive.

My prayer is that you will choose to support the symbolic starfish by choosing to live your life by the principles it represents. My prayer is that you will choose to, by living according to these principles, throw yourself into the life-sustaining ocean of the one who made you. The one who knows you better than you know yourself. The one who created the universe and all that's in it. After all, the word *uni* means "single," and the word *verse* means "spoken sentence." The Bible's very first words are "In the beginning, God created the heavens and the earth!" (Genesis 1:1, NIV). If God can speak the universe into existence, don't you think He can pick you up, as fragile as a little starfish, and return you to the "river of life" from whence you came?

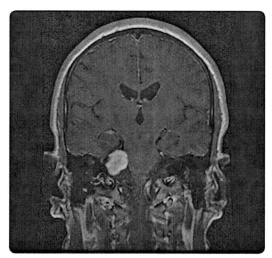
"Guy's MRI with the Acoustic Neuroma clearly visible"

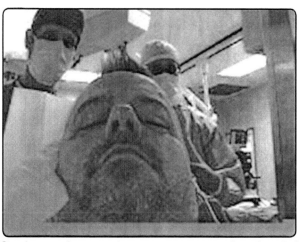
"Guy being taken into the operating room in Los Angeles"

"Guy's beautiful wife LaDonna"

"Guy and LaDonna the evening of their wedding day"

"Guy's son Austin and his fiancé Bre"

"Guy's immediate family"
front right to left – "Guy's brother Brad, father Arvis, mother Wanda"
back right to left – "sister-in-law Tami, wife LaDonna, Guy, son Austin"

"Guy's father Arvis Gene Smith"

"Guy with his son Austin at his Army boot camp graduation"

"Arvis and Wanda Smith celebrated 50 years of marriage!"

"Guy's family" front right to left "Guy's daughter Ansley, wife LaDonna, daughter Abigail, granddaughter EllaRose" back right to left "Guy, son Alex"

"Guy and his father, Arvis, on one of their trips across country"

"Guy's favorite picture of he and his daughter Ansley"

"The Howard Family" from left to right "mother Debbie, father Steve, sister Chelsea, Brooke, brother Hunter"

"Brooklyn Nicole Howard"

"Guy's granddaughter EllaRose"

"Walter"

The ARVIS Foundation

I would like to mention the ARVIS Foundation (www.arvisfoundation.org). This is a foundation that I have created to try to spread the word about the ARVIS Effect. The purpose of the ARVIS Foundation is to create a 501(c) 3 manner in which donations can be made in order to fund mission work in the USA. To assist in the travel expenses of performing Scream N' Shout, the Visiting Brooklyn anti-bullying assembly program, and other school programs, as well as a children's camp that I want to build.

Camp HERO (Helping Everyone Reach Others) is a camp that would allow kids who cannot afford to go to a Christian camp to come and learn about Christ, serve the community, commune with each other, and to have clean family fun for a few days or for a week. They would be brought to the camp free of charge via donations and money raised through the ARVIS Foundation.

Upcoming Books

THE SERGEANT is a fictional story of a young soldier's encounter with a Sergeant on the beaches of World War II. Frozen with fear, Private Travis R. Chambers has to make some decisions that would mean life or death! His chance encounter with an unknown Sergeant will forever alter his way of thinking and ultimately his life.

FIGURE AT THE WALL is the story on one mans glimpse into what took place during the three days that Christ was in the tomb. As an observer, this man was witness to one of the most amazing and awe inspiring scenes that could ever be told. This book will take you on a journey through Heaven and Hell as you bear witness to the Majesty, Power and Divine presence that is Jesus Christ!

BRIDGE TO LIFE is the story of a man with no way out. Pressures of life, family, career, and a total lack of Faith will drive this man to the brink of disaster. Facing the ultimate decision, this man comes across a simple piece of paper that will ultimately cause him to ask the question.."Is life worth living?"

CPSIA information can be obtained at www.ICGtesting.com
Printed in the USA
LVOW10s1153180916

505033LV00001BA/2/P

9 781682 708743